ABOUT THE AUTHOR

· · ·

ANGELA BALCITA received her MFA in nonfiction writing from
the University of Iowa. Her work has appeared in the *New York
Times*, *Iowa Review*, and *Utne Reader*, among other publications.
She lives in Baltimore with her husband and daughter.

MOONFACE

MOONFACE

• • •

A TRUE ROMANCE

ANGELA BALCITA

HARPER ● PERENNIAL

NEW YORK ● LONDON ● TORONTO ● SYDNEY ● NEW DELHI ● AUCKLAND

HARPER ● PERENNIAL

HarperCollins books may be purchased for educational, business, or
sales promotional use. For information, please write: Special Markets
Department, HarperCollins Publishers, 10 East 53rd Street, New York,
NY 10022.

Portions of this book first appeared in the *New York Times* and the *Iowa
Review*.

FIRST EDITION

Designed by Betty Lew

Library of Congress Cataloging-in-Publication Data

Balcita, Angela.
Moonface: a memoir/Angela Balcita.—1st ed.
     p. cm.
       ISBN 978-0-06-153731-8
       1. Balcita, Angela—Health. 2. Kidneys—Diseases—Patients—
Maryland—Baltimore—Biography. 3. Kidneys—Transplantation.
I. Title.

RC902.B28 2010
617.4'610592092—dc22

                                                              2010008606

11 12 13 14 15   OV/BVG   10 9 8 7 6 5 4 3 2 1

AUTHOR'S NOTE

· · ·

This is a work of nonfiction. It recalls events in my memory, which is not always the flawless machine I wish it to be. But what I do remember, I've reproduced for you here as accurately as I could. The names and identifying characteristics of some of the individuals in these pages have been changed to protect their privacy, though they should know who they are.

For Chris

MOONFACE

ACT I

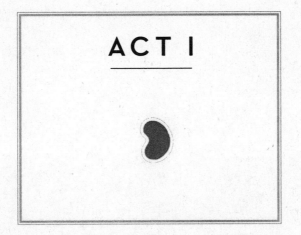

Chapter One

DIRECT from the LAND of FANTASTICAL SCENARIOS, the GREATEST and MOST SENSATIONAL TRAGICOMEDIANS in the WORLD

. . .

I TELL CHARLIE WE SHOULD AT LEAST GET OURSELVES SOME costumes. A fake mustache, a cane, a boa, some matching tuxedos. *Something*, I tell him.

"Don't get crazy, Moonface," he says. He looks at me and winks. His scruffy voice matches the stubble on his chin, and I'm in love with his eyes, which sparkle like diamonds even when his eyebrows get in the way.

I always tell him that I think the story could be better, that we could add fireworks, go to parties with roman candles in our pockets and light them up when the questions start flying. Or wear tap shoes and do a little kick-ball-change after every punch line.

"Are you kidding me? What we've got is gold, baby. Gold!" He grabs my face. He kisses me hard on my cheek.

Charlie is the showman. He's got the wit and the delivery. He can play to a crowd without the props or the fancy sets. If we really did have an act—I mean, one that we actually made money off of—he'd be the manager, the one calling the shots. And I'd let him. He has a way of telling a story and running with it.

"So, show us the scar you got from the surgery, man," someone from the audience will ask. The audience is usually our families and our friends. Sometimes strangers at parties.

Charlie lifts his shirt and says, "Surgery? What are you talking about? I got this baby from a shark bite when we were swimming off the deep seas of Palau. See the teeth marks?" He points to the little dots where the doctors had him in staples.

"Nawwww!" the crowd calls. Some of them gasp in horror.

"Come on, Charlie, tell 'em the truth," I interrupt. I furrow my brow and puff out my lips. Me? I'm all facial expressions. Charlie says I can change the mood of a room with just the look on my face. That, and I follow cues really well. "We got shipwrecked on that island and we tried to kill each other for food. See, I've got one, too. He tried to get me first, but I went straight for that white meat, if you know what I mean."

Then, I lift up my shirt to show the crowd my scar, also on my left side. And then we demonstrate what that stabbing might have looked like had we really done it. We take turns pretending to jab a knife into each other's stomach, over and over again.

"Aaaawww!" one of us yells.

"Aaaawww!" the other one yells.

It has our family and friends rolling in their sofa cushions for hours.

At first, we tried to tell everyone our story, all serious and sweet, how I have this disease, how he gave me his kidney, how I was in bad shape. The sacrifice, the pain, yadda, yadda, yadda. But even when we talk to our audience honestly about the transplant, we can't help but crack the jokes, because, as Charlie says, "How else are you supposed to look at life? *Seriously?*"

We have other acts, too, you know, and if I had my way, we'd be touring the cocktail party circuit headlining with my favorite one, the one where we call ourselves the smooth 1970s singing duo *Cocoa and Cream*. Tall, blond white guy and short, mocha-colored gal with dark hair, dark skin, flat chest, but nice ass, if I do say so myself, swaying softly in front of the crowd to the soothing tunes in our head. And just when the crowd thinks they've got us all figured out, Charlie points to his chest and says, "I'm Cocoa. She's Cream."

The crowd digs it. They laugh. They shake their heads thinking, "They're sly! Aren't they just sly?"

"Oh, Charlie," I say, smacking my gum and batting my eyelashes. Then he sings our slow, number one R&B hit into a make-believe microphone. *"I have this empty space way down deep inside me / And it's where my kidney used to be / And I can't . . . hold back . . . my love."*

I look out of the corner of my eye for my cue. He gives me a nod, and that's when I know my line comes, *"Ooooh, yeah, my love is soaring / Now, give me all your . . . vital . . . organs . . . yeahhhh . . ."*

See, that's how to win a crowd over. Not with the part about the blood transfusions and the dialysis or the medicine and the infections. Best to keep that stuff way down deep inside where the crowd can't see it, because if you think about that stuff here, you don't have much of a stage presence. In fact, you end up making yourself into a prop. The weeping willow. The bird that always sings the sad song. The crowd doesn't want to cry or to feel your pain. They want to crack the jokes right along with you.

Take Charlie's mother. I mean really, please take Charlie's mother. If she's in the crowd, she'll say something like, "Now after all this, don't you think you should be married by now?" She puts her hands in the air, looks at the audience, and shrugs. They nod their heads. "Yes, yes."

While it's not usually my M.O. to talk about this stuff in the middle of the act, the crowd gets to me and I say, "Yeah, Charlie. Listen to your mother. Why don't we get hitched?"

Then Charlie makes a long face, one that droops way down to his knees, and he says to the audience, "I give her my kidney, and she still wants my heart. Women!" He sighs.

If my brother's in the audience, he pitches in his two cents, too. "What? My kidney wasn't good enough for you? You still owe me for that, you know. I've got a guitar picked out."

"Save it, hon!" I say. "That's another story!" You see? Everyone's a comedian. We've learned to look past the hecklers and go on with the show.

"So, I give her my kidney, and she finally gets better and quits whining in my ear about how sick she is. *I'm so sick. I'm so sick,*" Charlie whines in a high-pitched nasal voice that is supposed to resemble mine, but I don't think it's anywhere close. "*Poor me, poor me.*" He pretends to cry, wiping his cheeks free of the tears. And right on cue, I put up my dukes and give him a shot in the arm. I always miss and stumble clumsily to the side, just like a good straight man should.

And that's how it goes.

And the crowd laughs.

And we're at the center of it all, the brightness shining on us like a big operating room light. Only this time, I'm laughing so hard, I don't feel any pain.

THE FIRST TIME I MET CHARLIE WAS AT A PARTY IN COLLEGE. BACK then, I was a shy Catholic girl with a pimply face and legs like needles. Charlie was smiling, drunker than a worm at the bottom of a tequila bottle. He was wearing a pair of those gold Elvis sunglasses with fake sideburns attached to them, sauntering up to every coed saying, "It's me, baby. Your hunk-a, hunk-a burnin' love." All the other girls ignored him, but I couldn't take my eyes off his curled lip and the way he swaggered when he walked, starting way down deep in his knees, and all the way up to his hips. *Boom, boom, step. Boom, boom, step.* When he finally came up to me, he took off his sunglasses, looked me straight in the eyes and said, "Priscilla, that you?"

I bet after that he thought it would be happily ever after, all jokes and silliness. All kissy face and googly eyes. I bet he didn't think he had a sick puppy on his hands. Early on, I tried not to bring it up. Instead, I let him buy me drinks. I laughed at all his jokes. I was afraid to tell him about my kidney disease and about the first transplant I got from my brother when I was eighteen. But he didn't seem to mind it. In a crowded bar, he held his chin up with one hand, and reached across the table to touch my arm with the other.

"I have three kidneys," I came clean.

"So what, I have a Spock ear."

"I mean, I take like nine medicines," I said.

"I get sunburned through skylights," he challenged.

"High blood pressure."

"Osgood-Schlatter."

"I have a big scar that runs from one side of my belly down to my bikini line," I confessed.

"I have . . . to see it!" he said.

Later that night, he did see my scar. He put his lips to it, flush against my distorted skin. He kissed me there and then all over.

Still, I didn't want Charlie to look at me and only see my medical history. I stuffed my blood-pressure cuff in a closet before he came over, and I stashed my medicines away in an inconspicuous basket over the microwave. But while standing in the kitchen of my college apartment drinking a beer one night, he leaned up against the counter and reached for one of the plastic orange pharmacy bottles and started reading the label out loud.

"Caution: May cause increased appetite and fat deposits. May cause acne, hair growth, weight gain, and a moon-face complexion," he read.

From a barstool, I looked down and focused on the tiles on the floor. I could feel the heat rise up against the sides of my face like a rapidly developing sunburn. He had picked up a bottle of Prednisone, one of my anti-rejection drugs with the ugliest side effect. It bloated my cheeks and rounded the shape of my face. I was a cartoon head atop a human body. This drug made it clear for everyone who saw me that I wasn't just a regular girl; it marked me as transplanted.

Charlie held the bottle and combed the stubble on his chin with his fingers. Then he said, "Moon-face . . . That almost sounds pretty, huh?"

I BET HE THOUGHT THAT'S ALL HE'D HAVE TO DO. MAKE ME LAUGH, fetch me a blanket when I got cold, drive me to the doctor's office when I needed it, say "there, there" every now and again. I bet he didn't think that after six years together, I would get sick again, and he would be the one to give me his kidney.

Now, after the surgery, everyone calls him the "hero." I am the one he saved. My mother introduces my brother and Charlie by saying, "This is my Hero #1, and this is my Hero #2." I look at it that way, too. But you know what throws me for a loop? Even now, Charlie calls *me* his Super Woman. "You and your amazing powers. They turn me on. *Grrrrrrrrr,*" he says, grabbing at the air with his hand as if it were a paw.

"What are you talking about?" I say. "I'm as weak as a baby."

"Nah, come on. You know what I mean." I think he means the risk we took. We were playing Russian roulette with this transplant, betting everything on our lucky number. My body could figure out that this kidney isn't really my own and start trying to get rid of it tomorrow. And while that risk is out there, it's much easier to suspend the belief that these things could happen, that Charlie's kidney is more like a superkidney, the exact remedy I need, and that with it, I may never be sick again. But even Charlie, often dupable and often a big suspender-of-belief himself, still thinks more practically when it comes to things like that. Like when he comes home and finds me throwing up into the toilet bowl.

"You okay?" he says, standing against the bathroom door. "Moonface, how can I help you? What can I get?" He looks like an angel to me, his blond curly hair against the hall light. I want to tell him that I'm fine, that as long as he's standing there, I'm going to be all right. *Just don't leave.*

"A minute, Charlie," I say, holding him off with my hand until I can regain my strength. "I already called the doctor. Probably something I ate. No fever. No pain. Nothing to worry about."

When I'm back in bed, he makes me tea and rubs my feet. "How's a skinny little thing like you get to be so tough?"

I have to fight for it, I think. There are moments when I see myself running with all my strength through some grand landscape of wildflowers. Or where I am flying off to some deserted island without first stopping to think where the nearest hospital is. There are moments when I picture myself as someone other than the person contained in this body. But there is always something that jolts me back to reality. A cold, an infection. My daydreams don't last. When it gets to be too much, my eyes well up and I say, in a voice that's weaker than I'd like, "Oh, no, Charlie, here come the faucets."

"Pretend I'm the sink!"

He comes closer to me. "Let it out, Moonface. Don't worry. You're stronger than you think. Really. You're like The Great Wall of China . . . The Rock of Gibraltar . . . Hercules . . . Mount Everest . . . The Acropolis . . . The Golden Gate Bridge . . . The Statue of Liberty . . ."

"Yeah, yeah, okay," I tell him. Sometimes he doesn't stop talking. My eyelids get heavy. I wipe tears off with my shirt. I just want to sleep, crash in this bed, and wake up somewhere else.

"And, Moonface, we're in this show together, for better or worse. I'm counting on you." Charlie says. He lays his head on my arm. His voice gets slow and soft, like he's getting tired, too. "You're my honeybee . . . my sugar pop . . . my ragamuffin . . . my special girl . . . my Asian orchid . . . my sweet cheeks . . . my apple dumpling . . ."

"Asian orchid?"

"Yeah, that's what I said, my Asian orchid . . . my Cleopatra . . . my brown sugar . . . my buttermilk biscuit . . . my raspberry scone . . ."

He starts to fade.

"My june bug . . . my pet Chihuahua . . ."

And I fall asleep, dreaming of him still calling me names.

Chapter Two

CHARLIE O'DOYLE'S EPONYMOUS VENTRILOQUIST DOLL and the DEBUT APPEARANCE of an OUT-of-TUNE ORGAN

. . .

IT SEEMS LIKE CHARLIE'S ALWAYS BEEN LOOKING FOR HIS straight man. A buddy, a pal, someone to keep around. He says that entertainment genes run in his blood, but I blame his comedic nature on religion.

Charlie's father was drafted during the Vietnam War in 1968, and when he came home, disgusted by the savagery of war, he converted from Catholicism to Quakerism so that neither of his sons would ever have to see combat. To this day, Charlie thanks his lucky stars for that decision, but he didn't always feel that way, because when he was eight years old, being a Quaker wasn't about being a conscientious objector. It just meant that he had to wake up on Sunday mornings to go to Quaker meeting.

Charlie figured out that faking illness was a whole lot better than sitting in silence on a wooden pew in an old brick house waiting for people to be moved by the spirit to speak. When his family took off for meeting, Charlie sat at home and watched TV. But it was Sunday, which meant that the cartoons weren't all that good. So, Charlie kept clicking through until he hit channel 45, where the TV station played old-time black-and-white movies. One morning, little Charlie O'Doyle sat up on his couch, ate sugar-free cereal, and watched Abbott and Costello arguing next to a hot dog cart. Bud was trying to get Lou to put mustard on his hot dog.

He insisted that mustard was made for the hot dog. Lou didn't agree. Bud slid the jar of mustard to him anyway. Lou slid it back, declaring that mustard made him sick. Bud conceded. But Lou? He didn't let it go, imagining a scenario wherein he eats the mustard, gets sick, loses his job, and is forced to abandon his wife and children. He poked his finger in Bud's face, accusing him for his family's future hypothetical suffering. Lou didn't back down either, raising his voice and pleading with Bud to please get his kids out of the future orphan asylum until, finally, Bud got annoyed, quit the chat, and waved off Lou before walking out of the scene.

Charlie was mesmerized, his mouth agape, as he watched the two men banter as if they were playing tennis with their words: the tall, skinny guy lobbing lines into the air and the short, fat guy slamming them down for winners. From that moment on, Charlie was changed, forever talking out of the side of his mouth like he had a cigar hanging from his lips, forever looking for someone to argue with about mustard.

His first attempt at finding a partner was to dally in the art of ventriloquism. The summer after he discovered Abbott and Costello, he asked his dear Aunt Wendy to buy him a ventriloquist doll. Somehow, Aunt Wendy found one and gladly obliged. It was a dangly wooden doll with a butt-cut hairdo and red painted-on freckles sporting a brown suit and a bow tie. Charlie named his doll "Li'l Charlie O'Doyle," sat it on his knee, and tried to slow down his own fast-moving lips whenever it was Li'l Charlie's turn to talk. But, being the gum-flapper that he was, Charlie just couldn't control their speed.

The next year, for his birthday, Charlie asked his dear Aunt Wendy to buy him a pet mouse. She obliged again, and Charlie named it Sergeant Keyknob. He had big hopes of carrying his new partner around in his breast pocket and coaxing the sweet, furry critter out to do tiny mouse tricks for a crowd: doing loop-de-loops around Charlie's finger, creating the illusion that it was crawling into one of Charlie's ears and crawling out the other. But that didn't work out so well either, as Sergeant Keyknob didn't turn out to be a sweet critter at all, but a vicious little blood-sucking vampire-critter who would bite strangers' fingers any chance it got.

But Charlie's deepest desires always kept him looking for his partner, even if it meant running away from home, which he almost did one day when he was eight. He put on his maroon plaid suit and a clip-on bow tie, packed a hard-shelled suitcase with his stuffed penguin collection, and started out the door.

"Where are you going?" his mother called from the kitchen.

"I'm running away," Charlie answered.

"But why are you dressed up in a suit?" his father asked, trying to hold back his laughter.

"Because I don't have a tux," he said, with a wink before walking out the door and sitting out on the front curb all day. Until dinner.

For most of his childhood, Charlie grew up on the western end of Maryland in a sleepy railroad town that overlooked the Potomac. His family moved there after living in Baltimore, upstate New York, and West Virginia. Charlie was only eight when his father told the family that they were moving to a house that sat at the top of a hill and way down below at the bottom was a river. Of course, Charlie didn't imagine there'd be a town in there somewhere. No, he imagined that their new house sat alone on a mountain, and if he were to open the back door and start rolling down the mountain's slope, he'd roll right into the water. That's just how Charlie saw the world: as his own amusement park. Why couldn't he open the back door and dive right in?

CHARLIE SAYS THAT SOME DAY IN OUR CHILDHOOD WE PROBABLY met, both our families traversing the same highways all along the east coast in our respective station wagons. Charlie says that at some point, we must have crossed each other at an arcade or a candy shop. But I tell Charlie I would have remembered if I saw an eight-year-old kid in a suit and bow tie.

My earliest childhood memories begin in Queens, New York, in the fourth-floor apartment of a horseshoe-shaped building on Yellowstone Boulevard, a broad street that ran through the borough. My father was a young Filipino doctor finishing up a residency at a nearby hospital. My father, my mother, my brother, and I lived in a two-bedroom apartment with bars on the windows and a front door that was crowded from floor to ceiling with locks. While most people would complain about sharing a room with their brother, I didn't mind it. While my father was gone, spending long nights on-call at the hospital, my brother was the one I idolized, the one who could play stickball and run down the street so fast that I'd have to call for him before he went out of my sight. He'd fly down those alleys fearlessly, careening around Dumpsters and telephone poles. "Joel," I'd yell, "waaaaait," my arms cupped around the sides of my mouth, my voice ricocheting against the tall buildings that tunneled a side street.

While he was the strong one, and the fast one, I was the skittish one. While he was growing bulges in his arms and slowly becoming able to help my father lift luggage and groceries, my features were always more delicate: bony elbows and sharp shoulders. "Just like Olive Oyl," my mother would say when she looked me over. "Maybe if you ate some spinach, you'd be stronger."

I sat out many of those stickball games, and often I stayed out of school for a stomachache or fear of an impending stomachache. I blame that fear on my father's precautionary mindset that, while trying to keep me safe, instilled great worry in a young impressionable me. His scenarios always shot straight for the worst: "Don't laugh during dinner or you will get indigestion and diarrhea." Or, "We'd better clean up that cut or bacteria will seep in and you'll get an infection. Then, you'll have to take antibiotics." One summer I told him that someday, I'd like to get a summer job at the local Baskin-Robbins, where those pretty older girls wore pink polo shirts. But my father closed the subject immediately. "Scooping that hard ice cream?" he said, looking at skinny wrists. "Carpal Tunnel Syndrome."

While I walked carefully through those early years in New York, my brother seemed untouched by my father's warnings. He threw his head back in total abandon and laughed at what seemed to be dangerous and confusing situations. I tried to follow his cues, tried to understand what was funny and what was not. For instance, according to my brother, Benny Hill, the fat, pasty Englishman in boxer shorts, was hilarious. I was a grade schooler, then too young to understand the innuendo between him and the other characters on his TV show—why he was an old man dressed in women's clothes, why the busty blonde behind him was scantily clad and hitting him over the head with a frying pan. My mother sat on our couch giggling with her entire body, pressing her hand on my brother's shoulder as if she could not contain herself anymore, as if she had to physically pass off the joy of the moment to someone else. I remember my brother trying to come up for air during those shows, laughter coming out of his mouth like horns blaring from a boat: *loud and then soft, loud and then soft.* But I sat still and watched.

But, then, one weekday afternoon, with the apartment windows open and the television on full blast, I heard Lucy's whiny voice on *I Love Lucy.* She cried like a baby one minute and squinted her eyes like a cunning mastermind the next. I sat on my parents' bed and watched as Lucy tried to keep up with a conveyor belt of nonstop chocolate drops. There she went, twisting her face and jerking her limbs as the belt turned faster, too quickly for her to hold the chocolate drops and wrap them in tissue paper. Panicked, she stuffed the chocolates down her shirt, under her hat, and into her mouth until her cheeks were full like balloons. Now *that* was funny.

I mimicked her antics in front of the mirror for the rest of the afternoon, pretending Lego pieces were the chocolates and sheets from a memo pad were the wrappers, then stuffing them into my shirt and under the Red Sox baseball cap I was wearing. Later that evening, when I tried to reenact the scene for my family, I stood in front of the dinner table and pretended it was a conveyor belt and that the popcorn shrimp were pieces of chocolate that I had to wrap, and I stuffed my face until my cheeks puffed out like a trumpet player's. I put them down my shirt and on top of my head.

"Ethel! Ethel!" I cried. When I looked up, my brother stared at me blankly.

My mother, so confused by the chaos, grabbed at my hands and said, "No, no! One by one!"

"You'll choke!" my father said.

• • •

INCREDIBLY, I GOT OUT OF MY CHILDHOOD UNSCATHED. THAT IS, until college, when it seemed that all my father's nightmares finally materialized. It began one day when Marsha, a big-breasted Italian girl, came into our dorm room and found me sitting on the edge of my twin-sized bed. She took one look at me and said, "Oh, my god, you're pregnant."

This was the beginning of my freshman year. October, to be exact. Just enough time for me to center my Pearl Jam poster perfectly over my bed, just enough time for an enormous pile of laundry to accumulate in the corner of the room.

Marsha was looking at my ankles, which, once perfectly chiseled, slipping into slim flat shoes with ease, were now swollen like two boiled potatoes.

"I'm not pregnant," I told her.

"If you don't think you're pregnant, then you should call your dad."

I knew I wasn't pregnant, and I knew I should call my dad, but I just sat on the edge of the bed staring at my feet. Earlier, when I came home from sociology class, I noticed that the short walk was suddenly longer, that the hill that led from campus up to the dorm was suddenly higher, and by the time I reached the front door, I was exhausted.

Marsha knew that I should call my dad, because her dad was a doctor, and my dad was a doctor, and overprotective dads like ours—hers Italian, mine Filipino—would want to know this. I had always had little things like this going on—a stomachache or a cold sore that my father could fix. By this time, my family had already moved to the suburbs of Pittsburgh, where we were far away from the bustling streets of the city. My school was only a few hours from home, and when my parents drove me down to Baltimore that first weekend, my mother insisted that I take a crucifix, while my father pushed a plastic box full of pills and elixirs clearly labeled MEDICINE into my hands. "Just in case," he said.

I kept checking my ankles to see if the swelling went down. It didn't. So, I called my mother and told her that my ankles were swollen and that I didn't know why, and she snapped back, *"Ay! I know why. You are drinking too much, anak. Stop drinking. It makes your ankles swollen, you know. It's a proven fact."*

I told her that I wasn't drinking that much, and that drinking did not lead to swollen ankles. "You don't know. You think you know, but you don't know. *Ay, anak ko!"* she said before giving the phone to my father, who had obviously been listening to the entire conversation.

"Do your ankles hurt? . . . How do you feel? Hot? Cold? Worn out? Do you have a fever? . . . Headache?" I answered no to all his questions, none of the symptoms he named striking a chord with me. Until he said, "Baby, are you out of breath?"

"Hmm, yeah," I said. "I was out of breath on the walk home. It was weird. And it wasn't even that far."

There was a long pause in his voice, the way my father pauses when he's turning something over in his head, like the time he couldn't figure out how to assemble our new mailbox post or like the time he got us lost in Washington, DC. Then he said, "Tonight, sleep with your legs up on a pillow. Call me tomorrow if they're still like this."

When I did call him the next day to tell him that nothing had changed, that, in fact, the elastic in my socks had made deep pits into my fat skin, he said two words: "Come home."

I heard the concern in his voice, but I didn't want to go.

I had recently gotten the attention of a particular boy in my philosophy class who was, for the most part, oblivious to my ex-istence. There were other boys who were looking at me, too, I think. Also, I had done my first beer bong and keg stand, without spitting beer out of my mouth like an amateur. More recently, I had obtained a decent, authentic-looking West Virginia driver's license from two guys in the next dorm over who had bought a gold-colored blanket for a picture background and invested in a laminating machine. With a good ID I could get into any Bal-timore bar I pleased within the five-mile radius of our sheltered campus, where the doormen—who were mostly seniors at my school—would take one look at the ID and then at my boyish hip bones and my fresh face and let me in anyway.

I didn't want to leave because it felt like my life was just beginning—a life in which I didn't worry what would happen if I stayed up late or if I stood outside without a coat. To relinquish such a status so early in the game, even for just one weekend, would offset any hopes I had for status or consistency, for mak-ing a name for myself in the partying world on campus.

I GOT A RIDE HOME THAT WEEKEND, NOT THE LEAST BIT CON-cerned about the state of my health. I knew my father could make the swelling in my ankles go away, just as he had so easily done with my other ailments in the past. As soon as I left campus, I was hurrying to get back.

"My *anak*," my mother said, pulling my head down to her chest as I walked into the house, not yelling now, but clinging to me and not letting go. My father pulled my feet up on the couch, looked at my ankles, and shook his head.

I began missing classes shortly after then, sometimes weeks at a time, as my father dragged me from one hospital to another, to doctors with blood pressure machines and needles and tongue depressors who told me to wait in the other room as they talked to my folks in private. I sat outside reading magazines, and when they came out and asked me if I had questions for them, I said, "Yeah—when am I going back to school?"

On car rides home, my parents yelled at me for not paying attention to the doctors, and told me to stop complaining about my puffy face and what the medications were doing to me. At the hospital, the doctors pulled my father aside in the hallway and said, "I think she's more concerned about the aesthetics of this disease than what's happening to her." I overheard that and thought it might be true.

I went back to school for a time, and then a result from my blood test required me to come home again. My dad drove down to Baltimore by himself this time, and picked me up and took me back to Pittsburgh. I stood in the parking lot waiting for him while girls walked by and said, "Going out tonight?"

I said, sadly, "No, going home," without an explanation.

This went on for weeks, all a blur for me, as I scrambled to get my missed assignments when I got back to the dorm, and as Marsha recounted the weekends for me, telling me who had hooked up with whom, and who had beat up whom, and I was so jealous of her and her big ballooning tits bouncing as she talked with her big Italian gestures.

Then, just when I got home for winter break, when I thought I'd finally have time to relax after trying to play catch-up all semester, a doctor with a thick German accent and a white lab coat brought us into his office. His eyes were warm and understanding across the table, and he spoke slowly. "You have *Glomerulonephritis*, which is a kidney disease. Your kidneys are failing, and now we're going to have to treat them. It may work with medica-

tion or may not. I don't know, but we're going to try our best."
He tried to make himself sound clear, but to me his words just
sounded vague and cruel.

So this was the point at which my higher education went
from learning about Western civilization, philosophical anthro-
pology, and basic bong hit methodology to taking a crash course
in applicable premed. Now, I sat up in hospital beds and people
pointed to anatomical diagrams of the kidneys, and showed me
how they regulated blood pressure, how they filtered the waste
from the body. It was the beginning of my father finally revealing
to us the world of medicine that he had kept from us for so long,
thinking that we simply weren't interested. When I had specific
questions, he explained my disease in a language that was logical
and plain. Curling his forefinger into his thumb to show me how
filters in the kidney worked, he said, "These filters in your kidney
are usually very small, but yours are big for some reason. They're
letting all the wrong things in and out of your body, and that's a
problem."

Prior to this, I was not dependent on numbers, measurements, and ratings, even though I had gone through twelve years
of schooling. But now I began watching as the nurses took my
blood pressure, and I learned to watch as the needle swept along
the scale before hiccupping at 200 or 220. It was the first time
I'd try to use my psychic powers to determine that number or
to lower it, begging that the needle move far down on the scale
before it began to hiccup and slow.

To my surprise, different things came more easily, like getting my blood drawn. I had gotten used to the smell of the alco-
hol pad that they smeared across my arm, and that quick prick
that followed. I watched as the blood spurted into the tube, and I
watched until the tube was full. These, I learned, were minor de-

tails in the process. The moment when I really needed to sweat? Waiting to see the reaction on the doctor's face when he came in to tell me the blood test result, about my creatinine level, the measurement for how well my kidney was functioning. And I was beginning to get used to his face cringing uncomfortably as he read the number: 2.5, 4.3, higher and higher every time, when I knew it should be less than 1.0. That 0.7 is normal.

This was not the beginning of my mother praying, or wrapping rosary beads around her hand, then tucking them under her sleeve and trying to be subtle about it (she had been doing that for as long as I could remember), but it was the beginning of her going to church daily, waking up at 7:00 a.m., and kneeling before God for an hour before coming into the hospital to see me. Near my bed she'd say, "Oh, *anak,* if I could only take this thing from you and put it in me, I would. That's what I pray for."

Over those weeks, my father's face grew permanently worried, sinking slowly from the lines in his forehead to the skin under his chin. His smile, which he usually flashed with ease, was now a struggle for him.

Buxom Marsha started calling me more frequently then, first with more stories and more assignments, but later to tell me that the boy in philosophy class whose attention I had recently acquired? Yeah, well, she was dating him now.

I held the receiver and thought that this was what kidney disease can do to you. It can make clear the things you stand to lose.

"Transplant," the doctor said, when I finally asked him how we could make this all end. I traced back into my memory what I knew of this word: baboon hearts, organs in coolers on helicopters.

The intern came in, her lab coat sagging with pocket-sized reference books. She held her hands against my hips and chest and asked, "Can I listen to your heart?"

"Sure," I said.

"You're a college student?" she asked. She wore braces and a ponytail and didn't seem much older than I was. "Taking time off from your studies?"

I nodded.

"Breathe deeply for me," she said, as she touched my shoulder blades. And I let out a slow deep breath.

"Well," she said, tossing her hair back and pushing her hand into my hips, "at least you're learning some anatomy." She laughed to herself, trying to make a joke out of all this. But it just didn't seem all that funny.

Chapter Three

The MOVIE CLASSIC
HOLY BROTHER of GOD,
COMPLETE with BEAUTIFUL
LIGHTING EFFECTS

. . .

LATER THAT SUMMER, I WOKE IN A HOSPITAL ROOM IN PITTS-burgh from a mid-afternoon nap. My mother stood over me with a half-empty plastic bottle shaped like the Blessed Virgin Mary. I thought to myself that somewhere in China there was a factory where small Asian women were melting plastic, pressing it into a mold shaped like Mary, pressing it again and letting it harden until her arms stayed outstretched without drooping or falling, and until you could see each individual fold in her gown. We always had little bottles like this around our house, and ever since I was little, I had always likened them to Mrs. Butterworth, also a woman in bottle form, a vessel for her own product.

My mother splashed me with Holy Water that she shook off her fingers with force, the way superheroes throw fire with their hands.

"It's getting in my eyes," I said.

"Then you close them," she said. She, in fact, had her eyes closed, and under her breath, she was mouthing a Novena.

I listened for the sounds in the hallway: someone wheeling a metal laundry cart, a nurse scolding a patient, a woman crying out in pain. I imagined that this was the woman I would be tomorrow, after they had opened me up, attached my brother's kidney to the wiring inside me, and sewn me back again. I would be the one waking up and screaming, holding my hand over my side.

A sharp pull in my hair, and I opened my eyes to see my mother pulling through the knots the way she sometimes pulled loose threads from the hem of a skirt.

"*Mom!*" I yelled, but she didn't stop.

The old loud hospital phone rang, shaking the movable table on which it sat. "Channel 3. Siamese twins who've never been detached, " my brother said. They had put my brother in another room and on a different floor, something about separating us to keep our names straight so they didn't have to switch the medications, and since our check-in, he had been calling me every time he saw something funny on TV. This time, it was a gross sight, really. On the wall-mounted television, there was one normal-sized woman, and attached to her at the hip (literally) was her sister, her smaller version. A side effect of sorts, clinging to her as they moved and talked. My brother had always been obsessed with the gross and absurd. *Ripley's Believe It or Not. Planet of the Apes.*

"How do they get dressed in the morning?" he said.

"Or go to the bathroom?" I asked him.

The things that made me retch were the things that enthralled him. Once, when we lived in Queens, he collected dead flies stuck in our bedroom window, and then took a needle and thread out of my mother's sewing box and made a fly necklace.

"Ow!" I yelled.

"What's wrong?" he said.

"Mom is pulling my hair out in large chunks."

"I'm not!" she yelled into phone.

"Tell her to lay off you."

"Lay off me!" I told her.

"Don't talk to me like that," she said to me, the line between her eyebrows deepening. She grabbed the phone from my ear and said the same thing to my brother, only, when he responded with something I couldn't hear, she laughed with him. He always won her over, though she didn't like to admit it.

A MEMORY: I STOOD ON A CHAIR IN OUR LIVING ROOM. A CRICKETY wooden one that sounded like it was going to pop under my feet. My brother's back was against the white-painted wall and his arms were perpendicular to his body. I was on the chair beside him.

He turned to me and said, "Now, you pretend you are a Roman soldier and nail spikes into my hands."

I looked down around the room "What nails?" I asked.

"Just pretend," he said. "Pretend like you're hammering nails into my hands."

"Oh, I can't do that," I said.

"Just pretend!" I could tell by the volume of his voice that he was getting annoyed with my ignorance, with my lack of imagination. "You're a Roman soldier, okay? I'm Jesus, okay? When they crucified him, they nailed his hands and feet to a wooden cross and let him hang there to die." By age ten, my brother was well versed in the New Testament. In religion classes, he paid close attention to parables and stories. At six, all I knew was that today was Holy Saturday and I was too sick to play outside. We were in our pajamas. My nose was running, and my head was hot, but he promised the crucifix game would be fun. The day before, he and my mother had watched the movie *Jesus of Nazareth*, staying up late while I fell asleep. He seemed to know what he was doing, so I followed him as he rescued me from boredom.

From my chair, I pretended to hammer a big spiky nail into his hand. He grimaced, and grunted painfully. "Oh," I said, easing up with my pretend hammer and pulling out a pretend nail.

"I'm just pretending," he whispered. "Keep going." He winked and nodded. "Now, you say, 'Jesus, King of the Jews, you shall die!'" He continued to feed me the lines. "Pretend to laugh as you do it. You know, 'Ha! Ha! Ha!'" He threw his head back with hearty laughter.

"Ha! Ha! Ha!" I repeated, throwing my head back, too.

He looked up at the ceiling and looked as if he could cry. "Forgive them, Father," he pled, "they know not what they do."

I was confused, not quite sure why I was laughing, or why I was nailing spikes into his hands. I looked up to see whom he was talking to, but all I could see was the bright yellow ceiling light. It shone over him, casting the shadow of his entire crucified body on the white wall.

A WEEK LATER, BACK IN RELIGION CLASS AT SCHOOL, SISTER MARY Victor's long navy blue habit was swinging low and heavy behind her. "Now, does anyone know who died last week?" She had one palm in the other as she paced back and forth. "I'll give you a clue," she said. "He is the King of the Jews. He suffered for our sins, and they nailed him to a cross. He died, came back to us, and then went up to Heaven. Does anyone know who this is?"

"Jesus!" someone behind me shouted out.

"That's right!" Sister Mary Victor cried.

It came to me like a puzzle. All the pieces started to make sense. "My brother!" I said aloud.

"Excuse me?" Sister Mary Victor snapped, her big eyes bulging and coming closer to me.

"Jesus Christ—is my brother! When I crucified him, he asked our father to forgive me!"

Sister Mary Victor gave me a long, cold stare through the thick lenses of her glasses, one that pierced straight through me and shrank me back into my seat.

"Well, *I* think he is . . ." I mumbled before I dropped my eyes toward the floor.

WHEN I GOT MY FIRST PIMPLE AT THIRTEEN, MY MOTHER TOLD me that when a girl gets a pimple, it means that she is secretly in love. Of course, I was—with some boyish face I can no longer recall. But her prophecy made me embarrassed, and I blushed. The stress of everyone finding out my secret made me worry even more until I broke out in full acne.

"Don't tell them that!" my father would say to my mother when she told my brother and me these things, but she never listened. While my father was a quiet Catholic who prayed privately, my mother was the one who believed that you got punished for your sins.

Throughout high school, there were times when I struggled with insomnia. I turned over and over again in my bed, paced the floor, and sometimes went downstairs to watch TV for hours before finally dozing off on the couch. I even tried praying. When I told my mother about it, she said that a deep-rooted guilt could keep someone awake for days.

"Something is on your conscience, isn't it?" she asked me,

squinting her eyes and trying to find the answer in my face. I flinched, and then I turned away. "You cannot sleep because you feel guilty. Am I right? Maybe you should go to confession," she whispered, her cold stare like that of a witch casting a spell.

I believed her. I told the priest everything I'd done. Everything: my secret crushes, my secret wish that the ceiling fan at church would fall down into the pews in the middle of Mass (just to make things interesting). I told him how, once, a friend dared me to steal purple mascara from the local mall. During the week, I kept a running tab of my offenses so I could confess them by week's end. I prayed every night; I listened to the gospels during Mass. My brother and I both did.

Every Sunday in church, I sat next to my brother, who sat next to my mother, who sat next my father, who sat by the aisle. Every Sunday, we stood, we knelt, we sang, and we prayed. Every Sunday since my First Communion, we all got up, stood in line, and took the Eucharist.

But one time it was different. I remember the loud dramatic sounds coming from the organ. They made our pews vibrate and made my bones shake. My brother was a high school senior, and between the weekly sermons, all he talked about was where he was going to college. I looked at his outfit. He had started wearing jeans to church, sweatshirts instead of button-down shirts. Lately, he had stopped singing the hymns, and he had started slouching in his pew while the priest was talking. My mother nudged him with her elbow and he shook her off.

When it came time for communion, everyone stood up and got in line. My brother, who didn't stand, held up this usually orderly process. He remained seated, leaving me stuck on the inside of the pew.

"Go!" I whispered.

"I'm not going," he said. He shook his head, put his feet up on the kneeler. I must have stood there with my mouth open, frozen by his protest. "No, I don't think I'm into it this week. You go." He moved his feet to allow me to pass.

I kept my eyes on him as I moved up the communion line. He slouched and looked around. He was confident in his decision. I was unsure of what was going on. I watched the other parishioners kneeling and praying. I wanted to yell at my brother right there from the communion line, "What are you doing? He's watching, you know!" But his body language was deliberately hostile, clearly stubborn. I took the Eucharist in my mouth, and prayed for my brother's salvation.

THE MORNING OF OUR SURGERY, I WOKE UP EARLY TO FIND MY mother yet again hunched over my bed. This time it was comforting to have her there. As the nurse wheeled me out of my room on a gurney and toward the O.R., my mother walked alongside, her hand trying to keep in constant contact with my arm, or my shoulder, anything.

"You pray!" my mother commanded, pulling a blanket over me before she left me with the nurse. I had been praying for weeks before the transplant. I asked God to make it work, to let me finally be okay, be done with the dialysis treatments, and get back to my life at school. Sometimes I sank to the ground on my knees and begged that the transplant would work.

Back in the room, balloons had filled the ceiling, and cards from well-wishers were stuck to every available surface of the wall. "Your courage is an inspiration," said one card with a cartoon lion drawn on it. *Fraud, fraud, fraud*, I thought to myself. Give me a choice, and I'll show you how "brave" I am. Give me the chance to open the door and run away from this whole disease, never have to deal with it again, and I'll show you I'm made of nothing but fast feet. I'm on automatic pilot. I'm reading the lines off the script and making the appropriate facial expressions.

But my brother? I didn't know what was keeping him there. He could have left any time he wanted and told everyone that he just couldn't do it, and no one would have hated him for it. They would've thanked him for trying.

ONCE, WHEN I WAS IN KINDERGARTEN, I RODE THE BUS WITH MY brother and his classmates, but he forbade me from talking to him. The girls in my grade sat in the back while he and his friends sat in the front. Only once do I remember him talking to any of us. There was one Korean girl, Jae-Bok, who had taken my finger puppet right off my pinky.

"Too slow!" she said and stuck out her tongue before stuffing the puppet into her jeans.

"Not fair!" I said. "Give it to me!" I must have said it loudly enough for my brother to hear because—bam! —just like that, an imaginary cape hovering behind his shoulders, he turned around in his green vinyl bus seat and said, "What happened?"

"Jae-Bok took my Piggy Puppet!"

"So!" she said, playing tough with my brother.

I wanted him to hit her, smack her in her place. But, foreshadowing the wit and insult comedy he will master in later years, my brother said, "Jae-Bok, you're a thief! You're a stealer! You're a Pittsburgh Stealer!" At the time, I hadn't caught how clever this was, how my brother linked up Jae-Bok's crime to a football team's mascot, especially since we weren't yet living in Pittsburgh.

But everyone else on the bus got it and hummed "ooooh," shaming Jae-Bok into returning the Piggy Puppet to me.

AN ORDERLY AND MY FATHER CAME DOWN INTO THE WHITE ROOM with Joel in a gurney between them. My dad came over to kiss me on the forehead and quickly made an exit.

"Don't be scared," he said.

Our stretchers were lined up along each side of the stark white hallway. Between us, nurses and orderlies shuffled by, flinging open the operating room door as they moved in and out. My brother, too, was clothed in white and had an IV running from his hand. I could tell by the flutter of his eyelids that the anesthesia was just starting to work.

I held my hand over the side of my waist where they would put in the new kidney, where they would transplant his organ into my body. There was an emptiness there now, like skin stretched over bone with a hollow space underneath. I tapped on it impatiently. I watched a nurse stand beside me, turning the pages in my chart. My eyes followed an orderly who came down the hall and repositioned my gurney so I was closer to the wall and out of the way of traffic. He tugged on my blanket to cover my exposed foot.

The double doors swung open one more time, and inside the room ahead, trays with equipment were rolled from this side to that. One nurse called out directions and another one adjusted the tube of my IV. I looked at my brother on his narrow gurney. He was dozing in and out of sleep. I felt my pulse, the tremble of my skin. The lights from the other side of the double doors seemed brighter and stronger than they were minutes ago. They seemed to come right over my brother, over his long white figure, his outstretched arms, his long legs. They illuminated his entire body.

THREE WEEKS AFTER THE TRANSPLANT, EVERYONE WAS FINALLY able to rest. My daily blood tests read that my brother's kidney was working, that my body wasn't rejecting it. I thought about how, before long, I would have to go back to Baltimore for school.

Friends and family called to ask how I felt. I didn't know how to tell them without jumping out of my seat. I felt the blood pumping in my veins and the breath in my lungs. I thought, *today I could run a hundred miles without stopping.* The scar over my abdomen was healing, and I wanted to eat all my favorite, salty foods that I was forced to avoid when my kidneys didn't work. I was someone else now. Someone better.

People came to see my brother and me and told us that even our parents were looking better, how the wrinkles on their brows had finally smoothed out. They were laughing again and the secretary in my dad's office confessed to me that she had finally seen my dad's big smile for the first time that summer. Not only was the transplant successful, but we had been living under the same roof for the past few weeks, and that made it easier for my parents to watch over us.

It just kept getting better after that. Three weeks after the transplant, I was restless and eager to use my energy. I needed a project. I didn't want to just sit around. The owners of the house before us had covered the entire second floor with cheap, ugly carpet. Underneath lay shiny, flawless parquet. My mother had been saying for years how she wanted to rip up that carpet, but she never did it. One day they came home, and I had rolled up half the carpet so that a big lump sat in the middle of the room.

"What do you think you're doing?!" they yelled.

"I was bored. It's not as hard as it looked. It wasn't bolted in there or anything." I had ignored my surgeon's orders to rest, and my father made me check my incision to make sure nothing had popped. I had the energy of a horse. That was what the new kidney did for me.

In the room across the hall, things were quiet. My brother was back in his childhood bed. His boxes from moving out of his place in Boston were piled up around him. Sometimes he came down to watch TV, whizzing through the channels impatiently. He was cranky because of the pain of his incision, a cut that extended from the front of his torso, around the side of his body, and all the way to the middle of his back. The surgeons warned us that the surgery would be more difficult for him, and I don't know if he ever believed that. If he didn't before, he did now.

"Do you want to go to the mall?" I asked him.

He stared back at me for a few minutes before I remembered that I wasn't allowed to drive for two months, he for three. We were stuck in that house until our parents got home.

I hadn't heard his laughter in a long time, despite how much I tried to egg it on. "Look," I pointed to the TV, "botched-up plastic surgery stories on channel 4." But instead of paying attention, he put on his earphones and tuned out.

HE HAD LOST TOUCH WITH HIS FRIENDS IN BOSTON AND DECIDED he would not return after he got better.

"Why not?" I asked. All I could think about was moving into my dorm in a few weeks and being surrounded by friends.

He responded with just a shrug and then went upstairs again to hide in his room. When my parents came home, I called him down for dinner, but he didn't respond and stayed up there for the rest of the night.

In the weeks before school, I should have been exhausted from my days of jumping around the house energetically and my newfound hobby as a carpet remover, from packing my boxes and planning my schedule. And while I was a little tired, I had trouble sleeping. After the transplant, I lay in bed trying to close my eyes and doze off, but I couldn't. I stayed up all night rolling from one side of the bed to the other, sitting up in the dark, and pacing the floor, trying to make out the millions of thoughts clouding my head, but the only words that came through were *forgive me, forgive me, forgive me.*

Chapter Four

DIRECT from SAN FRANCISCO: TWO DANCERS BALANCE ONE-FOOTED on the MOVING EARTH

• • •

I TELL CHARLIE I WAS A REAL DRAG BEFORE HE CAME ALONG, and he says to me, "Nah, Moonface. You just needed someone to find that spark in you." He says he was intent on lighting that spark from the first moment he laid his baby blues on me.

But I was skeptical. After spending the summer watching my brother slowly heal, I went back to school trying to pick up where I left off. I drank at the bars with my friends, but stopped after they were all too drunk to realize that I was nursing my drink and being more conscious about what I was taking in. I was keenly aware now that something had changed, that things did not go my way. Even when Charlie came along, I didn't believe him. The last thing I needed was to deal with a guy who thought he was the incarnation of Elvis. I was even reluctant about making a big move to San Francisco, but before I knew it, I was there, and I was waiting to meet Charlie.

I stood in that lobby in San Francisco waiting. Any minute now, Charlie would come walking out of that elevator. Then what? Shallow hug? Fidgety handshake? The flowers in the hotel lobby were fake and gray with dust. A bellman wearing gold tassels on his shoulders stood by the door and seemed embarrassed. Any minute now.

I sat on the green velvet couch and stared at the elevator doors. This was like when you dream about someone in your office and then the next day you're at the copy machine and that person is standing next to you asking you how long you're going to be, when just last night the two of you were rubbing the insides of each other's thighs and sucking on one another's ears.

It was the late '90s, the dot-com era, and I was working as a secretary for a computer company, and sometimes when I rode the bus from work up to Haight Street, I shut my eyes and saw glimpses of Charlie—him pumping up my bike tire, him helping me with the grocery bags and insisting on the heavy ones with the laundry detergent and the milk while I carried the chips and the t.p. But, when I opened my eyes, I remembered that a year earlier, I had said goodbye to Charlie on a rooftop in Baltimore. After our first kiss months before at a party, there was another party, and another upon our college graduation. Charlie and I sat for long hours on the benches outside the soccer house and talked, but when I rationalized it all, we were just a fling, an end-of-the-year romance. Besides, I had already made other plans to move out west. I had people waiting on me. I didn't stop thinking about him, though, not on the road trip out here, not when I dated a sleazy bike mechanic with an Asian fetish, and not when he called and left a message on my machine telling me he was in San Francisco for a convention.

•   •   •

ALL WEEK LONG SAN FRANCISCO HAD BEEN SO HOT—SO HOT that when you walked outside, old men on the sidewalk with brooms actually said, "Hot enough for you?" and still expected you to laugh, but you couldn't because you were so damn hot. After I first moved there, I learned to carry a sweater around, even in the summer, because despite San Francisco's California image, days there could be chilly, downright cold in July. But that week, bike messengers rode without shirts on. Businessmen fried in their suits. When I came back from my lunch break on Tuesday, Alex, the moody overweight IT guy in my office, a person I would never dream about, stood outside the lobby smoking a Camel. "You know what this is, don't you? It's earthquake weather. Yeah, I've seen this before," he said, his big chest inflating as he inhaled. Sometimes Alex could really be an idiot, and so often I tried to ignore him. But when I looked up to the sky, it looked green. Green where there should be blue.

After graduation, I packed up the car and moved there for the same reason a lot of people move to San Francisco—because it is far from home and because it is so mysterious. It was far from the east coast, where everyone seemed so obsessed with what kinds of high-powered jobs we would be getting with our degrees and when we were going to finally find a mate to marry. As soon as some friends and I rolled over the Bay Bridge, it seemed like no one was asking us those questions anymore. Instead, we sat in colorful apartments and talked about how wonderful the city was, how everyone was so nice. How the air smelled healthy. How when you woke in the morning and looked out the bay window of your tiny studio apartment, you felt full of possibility. I understood the feeling, but I didn't know what was possible yet.

I had planned to leave right after graduation. But when I told my parents of the plan, they made their positions clear: "no!" My mother said it, repeatedly and quickly while shaking her head, "NONONONONONO," so as not to put any room between the "no"s for me to interrupt. My father, on the other hand, said it once, clearly with both his hands and his eyes, before turning around and walking out of the room.

So instead of going straight to San Francisco right after graduation, I waited. I moved back into my parents' house and all summer long I stomped around the house, talking back, whining, acting like a child, because that's how they were treating me after all, right?

By August, my mother was so sick of my complaining, she yelled, "Okay, fine. Go!"

But don't think her dismissal came without her transferring her own paranoia into me. As she folded my laundry and pushed the sweaters into my overstuffed suitcase, she said, "Lock your door, *anak*, because people will open your door and suffocate you with your pillow in your sleep and steal all your things. Don't wear short skirts when you have to walk up the stairs, because men will look at you from below. Don't go anywhere at night. Just stay home. You know what people do. If you have a drink, they will slip a pill in your drink, and they will rape you. It's true. So keep your drink covered with your hand, like this . . . that way, no one can slip things in there. Don't tell anyone your phone number. They can track you down like that; they will know where you live."

And even though I knew that her fears came directly from the mouths of Diane Sawyer and John Stossel, her words still stuck with me, and made me think twice about everything, about living on my own, about if I could do this. My mother scared the shit out of me. But by the time our first rent check was due, I was stern with my landlord on the phone when he tried to stick us with a plumbing bill. At night, I walked around the city, and I knew how to take the well-lit streets. I gave tourists directions. At bars, I drank from beer bottles with skinny openings, but sometimes I set them on the bar while I reached for some cigarettes. I slept soundly in my apartment. Then one night . . .

WHAM!

My bedroom window smacked against its own frame. The wall moved closer to the couch I was sitting on.

It wasn't at all like I had imagined it would be, not at all like the earthquake simulation ride at Universal Studios. Nothing like this. It was more like a slap across the face, or a fender-bender. It was over before I realized what happened.

My roommates and I, all east-coast girls, didn't know what to do or how the shoddy walls of our apartment were going to hold up. We had to get out! I remember my friend giving directions as we walked out the door. "Walk on the side of the street where there are no buildings," she said, words that seemed so wise then. *Yes*, I thought, *so things don't fall on us.* So that's what we did, me and my roommates, practically crawling out of our apartment and up the sidewalk of a nearby park, far from the sidewalk and windows. The three of us stood in the grass in Alamo Square, trembling with fear, tears streaming from our faces. We waited for aftershocks.

When I looked up, the streetlights were still lit all along Hayes Street. The orange bus pulled along its cables and made small, electrical crackling noises as it made a usual stop on Divisadero and kept rolling on. People in restaurant windows were sipping soup from soup spoons. It was as if nothing happened. And the three of us, three girls from east of the Mississippi, sat alone atop Alamo Square and laughed into one another's shoulders.

When I got on the bus for work the next day, I clenched my body each time we jumped a pothole, or anytime the cable wires snagged and jolted out of place. We rode up and down the hills of San Francisco, but it felt like at any moment the earth below would split open and deep crevasses would swallow the bus whole. I hugged a pillow over my head at night, and went over an escape plan to myself: grab the walls for balance, slide down the stairs, and run out into the side of the street where there are no buildings. I didn't tell my mother about the earthquakes, lest she realize that this was an everyday danger and force me to come home. It felt like I was flailing in the city, scared of the next fault line to awaken.

I tried to hide any sense of anxiety I had when I went out with my friend Danielle, while we were out looking for boys to date. But once, when we sat in a bar and the ceiling thudded from the dance floor upstairs, the lights above the bar flickered, and I grabbed Danielle's hand as she drank her beer.

"No. You're fine," she said. She was the only native San Franciscan I would ever meet my whole time there. She told me to do something she learned in grade school as soon as I felt an earthquake coming: *stand under the door.*

THE GOLD ELEVATOR DOORS FINALLY OPENED, AND CHARLIE walked out into the lobby.

As soon as he saw me, he demonstrated his wingspan and he shouted, "It's the Incomparable Moonface!"

The bellboy and some guests looked over, but Charlie kept his bright blue eyes straight on me. He looked freshly showered, his curly hair shorter and darker than I remembered. When he leaned down to wrap his arms around me, his neck smelled like soap.

• • •

As we walked out the revolving doors and into the city, Charlie said, "San Francisco is hot!" He said the convention was boring. After school, he had started working for a trade show company that sent him to different cities to register the presenters and attendees. He said that the entire expo center was filled with booths of people talking about concrete and asphalt and construction supplies. He talked and talked, and I watched his lips move, his hands gesture; once, I touched his sleeve to feel the fabric of his blue button-down shirt. Good old cotton. Thick and reliable.

"God, I can't believe I haven't seen you since graduation," he said, "when you had that butterfly pinned to your cap, remember?"

"You remember that?" I said.

Columbus Avenue was thronged with people, but we twisted our way up the sidewalk, the fading sun on our backs, and walked into a bar and headed straight upstairs to the balcony. From our small cocktail table, we could see straight down into a sea of drinkers waiting for the bartender's attention, bills in hand and waving. There was a deranged, dirty guy with a patchy brown beard yelling about the war and our boys in Vietnam. I tried to ignore the smell of urine, but I couldn't.

What came after this? How do you continue where you had left off? In my imagination, Charlie had come all this way to tell me he was thinking about me, that he couldn't stop thinking about me, that San Francisco kept pulling him and pulling him. But after the small talk was over, and after we ordered our drinks from a strung-out waitress with fidgety hands, we became quiet, the distance between us vast.

After the drinks came, after the old man stopped his tirade

about Nixon, after several bar orders were called out down below, Charlie leaned in close, and in a deep, slow, serious voice said, "Can you name the countries of Central America?"

"What?" I said.

"There are seven. Can you name them?" Charlie put his beer down and looked at me directly. He came two thousand miles to ask me about geography. He was waiting.

"Um, Honduras," I said.

"One," he held up his index finger.

"Uh, El Salvador? Guatemala?"

"Yeah . . ."

"Belize . . . Nicaragua . . ." I was trying to picture the oil-cloth map in my memory, the one Ms. Wesner had pulled down from the top of the blackboard. "Costa Rica . . . How many is that?"

"Six."

What am I missing? I whispered to myself. I looked at the ceiling. The wood in the old bar was cracking. I suddenly became worried about how seismically safe the structure of the building was.

"The last one?" Charlie said, leaning in closer now, expecting brilliance.

"Not Uruguay, not Paraguay . . . Okay, tell me."

"Pana—"

"Right! Panama! Was this a test?"

"No. I just know these facts. I just know them. All these things that I know, I have to figure out a way to use them. You did good. What things do you know?"

"I don't know anything."

"So what kinds of things do you think about when you walk down the street?"

"Yesterday, I walked down the street singing a song I had just written."

"Really? Well, sing it."

"You wouldn't like it."

"No, tell me." He slumped his shoulders a little, and slanted his head to one side.

"It's stupid."

He looked at me. His invitation was irresistible. Quietly, I sang, *"Parking Meter, Parking Meter, glad to meet ya, Parking Meter, hate to feed ya, Parking Meter, love to beat ya, Parking Meter."*

Blank face. Dead eyes.

"I know; see? You asked."

"No, I like it."

"I was walking to work, and I was looking up at the top of a building, and slammed right into a parking meter. Clocked my chin. It's got a faster tempo than that. Very staccato."

"I love it," he said.

"I've got another one."

This time I sing with slightly more vibrato. This actually has a good melody. Think show tunes: *"I like you / in an inner tube / strategically placed / right below your waist. Get it?"* I jump out of my chair and stand in front of him, motioning around my hips with my hands like I have a spare tire around me. "It's a love song."

"Is there more to it?" Charlie said.

"I don't think so."

"How 'bout: *I like you / with a popsicle stick / cherry red / the kind I like to lick.*"

"Naughty!" I said. "I love it. And we could have models come out while we sing, dressed up like popsicles."

"You're funny, Moonface," he said, lifting his glass to his smiling lips.

The drunk downstairs was saying something about bombs. *"Bombs!"* he yelled.

THAT WEEK, THE HEAT BURNED OFF THE FOG THAT NORMALLY hovers over the city. You could see Sausalito clearly from Crissy Field; you could walk on the Golden Gate and see clear down to the water. From Twin Peaks, you could take in the entire city, white and clean, a landscape with the houses staggering on top of each other, a pincushion full of pins. But the sky still seemed green. It seemed to even tint the bay.

Charlie and I spent nights in his hotel. We lay close and tight, and in the morning, Charlie put on a suit and tie and walked to the convention center. I went to work and thought about Charlie all day. On the bus, I was having that familiar feeling again—as I stood and hung onto a rail, I couldn't place my feet. They seemed to move without me, jumping off my legs every time the bus skipped or hopped.

We walked all around the city. After Charlie talked on and on about how wonderful the city was, how boring Baltimore could be, I got the nerve to say, "You should just move here. There are tons of jobs," as nonchalantly as I could, looking into a store window as I said it.

"Hmm," he said.

We walked to North Beach and had dinner in a romantic restaurant with a purple neon sign in the window. He ate spinach ravioli and I had tiny meatballs covered in sauce. And we talked until the burgundy puddles at the bottom of our wine glasses drained and faded.

• • •

THE NEXT MORNING, IN HIS HOTEL ROOM, HE PACKED UP HIS things, rolling up his neckties and squeezing them into the side pockets of his backpack. I was about to leave for work, going in with the same clothes I had worn the day before, and planning not to be apologetic about it. I sat on the bed pouting. I wasn't going to be apologetic about that, either.

"You shouldn't leave," I said.

"I don't want to leave. I want to see you again," he said, sitting on the bed now, close to me. "I want to see you all the time. I would like to kiss you in the morning and in the night," he said. And I knew something was happening now, something. And I knew that as we stood at the door to his room, and he offered to walk me all the way to the lobby, but I told him, no, no, right here. He gave me a long, slow kiss, his hands on my hips, squeezing tightly, all ten fingers, as we stood in the doorjamb, my feet pigeon-toed and between his. I squeezed him, too, hanging on tight, and I swear I felt the earth moving.

Chapter Five

A SPLENDID COMBINATION
of PHYSICAL and SPIRITUAL RENEWAL
SET in the LOW and HIGH LANDS
of IOWA

. . .

CHARLIE AND I ONCE DROVE A RENTED BLUE AND ORANGE moving truck halfway across the country. It was a rattling tin can of a thing that threatened to snap in half at every pothole. The greasy-haired man at the truck rental office in Pittsburgh had handed us an awkwardly oversized atlas and said, "Iowa, eh? I don't even know where that is."

"Me neither," I'd said.

As we rode along on the sticky vinyl seats, I opened up the atlas to see the United States sprawled across the centerfold. And there was Iowa, smack dab in the crease of the page. A lavender rectangle underneath a loosely hanging staple. It connected six other states with its dotted border.

"Iowa. The place where things come together and fall apart," I said as I ripped the staple out.

"See, now that's beautiful. You should be writing this stuff down," Charlie said with a finger in the air and his eyes steadfast on the road.

But I wasn't trying to be poetic. I was trying to figure out how we got here. Ever since Charlie moved with me to San Francisco, we'd been hopping around from one city to another taking any small jobs we could find. We ended up in Pittsburgh in an attic apartment of a whitewashed brick house. I was doing temp work, shuffling around papers and answering phones at the headquarters of a bank. Charlie worked at an after-school program, helping at-risk kids with their homework and teaching them how to shoot penalty kicks. He wasn't exactly sure what they were at risk of, because for him they were enthusiastic and polite and laughed at every single one of his knock-knock jokes. He didn't mind the work, even though the government technically classified it as "volunteering" and his salary was a few measly paychecks and monthly food stamps. We used my paycheck to stock the house with milk, bread, pasta, and paper towels, and we used the food stamps to buy prosciutto di Parma and imported olive oil from the international markets downtown, because, as Charlie said, even if we were poor, we didn't have to lose our sense of taste. I agreed, but as I stood in line in the market holding a block of pecorino romano cheese behind a mother who was holding her two-year-old and a nine-can pack of tuna, also paying with food stamps, I thought, "We've got to get ourselves some real jobs."

"We're like vagabonds," Charlie'd said. "We just need to find our niche." He started thinking up ideas, and every once in a while he'd spit one out. Like once, when we were watching a PBS documentary on Peru. We spent an hour looking at those chiseled mountains and green landscapes before Charlie said, "We should be alpaca farmers!"

"It can't be that easy," I said. "PBS is pulling the wool over your eyes!"

Another time in a surf shop in Santa Cruz, he stuffed himself

into a full-body wetsuit, came out of the fitting room, and announced: "We're moving to the Bahamas! We'll have a synchronized swimming routine with the dolphins!"

I put a hand on my hip and said, "Are you trying to make me
laugh on porpoise?"

Another time, he stopped dead in the middle of the sidewalk,
turned to me and said, "I know, I know—a dinner theater slash
bowling alley."

"Spare me," I said.

THE IDEAS KEPT COMING, BUT THE NICHE NEVER MATERIALIZED.
Then one day, sick of waiting, I stood up from the couch and said
to Charlie, "I've got to find myself some meaning!"

"Religion?" he asked, looking a little worried.

"No," I said. "School." I bet Charlie was thinking clown school
or acrobat school, but I was thinking more like writing school.
"Stories, you know, of the bookish nature," I told him.

"So, you want to be a book writer?" He paused for a second,
looked down at the coffee table, and then he said, "Well, at least
you're using your imagination." It wasn't too much of a surprise.
We were both writing majors in college. I wrote long, obsessive
profiles about the boys I had crushes on; Charlie's stories always
baffled readers with the surreal. An odyssey about the boy who
thought he was the embodiment of time. "I was smoking a lot of
pot back then," he once confessed.

In Pittsburgh, I had been writing essays about my childhood
or about my and Charlie's adventures around the country. I com-
piled a few of the ones I liked, slid them into brown craft-paper
envelopes, kissed the seals, and sent them off to graduate schools.
At the end of spring, after all my graduate applications came back,

I told Charlie we were moving to Iowa, and the hairs of his curly eyebrows straightened out and stood up in full attention.

It just figured that Charlie would be excited for Iowa. It was like an empty canvas. It was unknown, unexplored territory, and with no obligations tying him to there, maybe he thought he could find his calling. But, as we finalized the moving details and bought new furniture, the more apprehensive I became. It took me hours just to decide on a couch. I was like a pendulum in the showroom, moving back and forth between the hulking uphol-stered beige beast and a spindly off-white loveseat that was sleek and easy to disassemble and pack.

"This one is crap," Charlie had said, kicking the loveseat's skinny wooden legs. "Let's just get the sofa."

"Ugh," I'd said. "But this one's so ugly. And it's heavy. And it's beige." I tried with both arms to lift it on one side, but it would not budge.

"This one will last us for a while," Charlie said.

"But what if we're sick of it in a year? What if we can no longer stand the beige?"

"Moony," he said, sitting back on the beige cushion and put-ting his legs up on a glass coffee table. "It's not like this is the last couch we'll ever buy."

"Yes, Charlie, but it's the *first* couch we'll ever buy. This isn't a futon we're finding on the street or a hand-me-down from my brother. This is ours; shouldn't we love it?"

"You're reading way too much into this," he said, as he called the salesperson over. He didn't balk until we went to pay for the sofa, doing a double take at the total before saying, "This is the most expensive thing I've ever bought in my life."

It wasn't just what we were bringing to Iowa that worried me; it was also the place itself. Even though Charlie and I had seen almost all the states as we traveled back and forth across the country, I only remember seeing Iowa in glimpses. Flat lines of green that halved the windows. Nothing stopped here, not even the wind, which carried everything past these roads and swiftly through the plains and didn't stop until it happened upon a mountain. After six years together, we chose this place to stop and put down our heavy furniture. What if Iowa could not entertain us? What if we got bored with it? With each other? I thought of Iowa as a stop on I-80 to get a quick bite before hopping back on the road, not as a place to plop down and stay a while.

As we drove along in the shaky truck, the east coast far behind in our rearview, I looked out the window and shook my head. But Charlie kept saying, "You're not looking closely enough. There are beautiful things here." He pointed out places on the side of the road where creeks cut into the grass to shape a valley and where a hill rose out of nowhere. "Like the hips of a woman resting on her side," he said, a smiled slathered across his face.

"*You* should be writing this stuff down," I told him.

WE MOVED INTO THE BOTTOM FLOOR OF A SPLIT-LEVEL DUPLEX. It was a cozy little joint with the windows posed high on the walls inside, but from the front of the house, they sat low and level with the ground. The hedges on the front lawn shaded the living room like natural curtains. Charlie and I hung our silkscreen posters of San Francisco up on the wall and placed plants in the corners of every room. While we felt snug there, the topographical positioning of our home disturbed my mother when she visited that summer.

"In the basement?" she said, her jaw dropping wide as if she were catching flies. She came in through a narrow entrance in the mudroom and walked beneath the low ceiling in the hall. I thought she'd like the compactness of the apartment, seeing as how she took up very little vertical space herself. "Why the basement?"

"It doesn't feel like the basement. Look how much light comes in. The walls are clean. No water damage." I pointed to the snow-white ceiling, the corner where we had stacked books alphabetically on a low shelf.

"But the basement?" she said, no less disgusted. She pointed with her chin to the hedges. "Close those windows. Aren't you breathing in the dirt? Come"—she reached for my arm and slung her purse over her shoulder—"we'll find you a new apartment."

But I liked the way the sunlight came in through the bushes outside. The street we lived on was so quiet that we could hear the thin tires of a passing bicycle rolling over the pavement. The town was bright during the summer and fall, and the sidewalks were sprinkled with wispy trees with bicycles leaning on them. Undergrads lived loudly in small farm homes or they crapped up bigger, nicer houses by putting frayed, busted-out Goodwill recliners on handcrafted, hundred-year-old wraparound porches. These details were offset by more charming parts of the community: the family-run hardware stores, the food co-op, the bookstore. Charlie and I took long walks along the perimeter of town, where the grass was high and the horizon was a sharp line at the end of a cornfield. And sooner or later, I began to see those little dips and bluffs in the earth, where the land seemed to be moving.

School was not the shocking plunge into cold water that I thought it would be, either. It was intimate midday discussions about writing and literature around wooden conference tables. It was potluck dinners at friends' houses and evening lectures at the local bookstore. The most worrisome part of my first year was the teaching, a requirement of my fellowship. I was assigned to teach rhetoric to freshmen, and the minute I was assigned the course, I found myself secretly cracking open my Webster's dictionary and looking up what the word "rhetoric" actually meant.

"You kind of don't have to know what it means," a woman named Beth said. She stood under a pavilion at the "Welcome New Grad Students" picnic holding a plastic cup filled with lemonade. I had been talking to her for most of the afternoon. "Trust me; you really don't even have to like teaching."

Beth was a year ahead of me in the program and didn't seem to mind me asking her question after question. She just sat there in her peach loose-fitting tank top, hiking shorts, and the sensible shoes of a librarian. She had dark brown hair and exotic yet indecipherable features; I'd later learn that she was half white and half Korean. I had the feeling she was quiet and shy, even though she greeted almost everyone at the picnic with an obligatory smile. Every once in a while, I caught her rolling her eyes when someone she didn't care for passed by. I could tell she hated teaching.

"So, what am I supposed to do? Should I just pretend like I am an authority on public discourse and debate? Those kids will see right through me," I told her.

"Listen," she said. "Your job is to go in there and jump up and down about rhetoric. Yay, rhetoric!" she said, shaking imaginary pom-poms with her fists.

Charlie concurred when I talked to him about it later. "She's probably right. Teaching is probably a lot like show business. You just have to keep them entertained. If you're excited about it, they'll probably get into it, too."

On the first day of class, dressed in a skirt to make me look older and in heels to make me look taller, I looked out into an audience of twenty freshmen and told them that rhetoric was going to change their lives. "Look at all it has done for me," I said, smiling and gesturing grandly with my hands. "A finely worded statement of purpose gained me admission into this school, my persuasive verbal skills and body language nabbed me a boyfriend, and with my captivating oratory, I have twenty new friends who are excited about rhetoric." It sounded silly coming out of my mouth, but no one thought it was funny enough to laugh.

"Please stop," I heard someone in the back left whisper.

FALL CAME AND WENT FASTER THAN I IMAGINED IT WOULD. I HAD been so busy with schoolwork and weekend dinner parties that I hadn't noticed the weeks flying by or the air getting cooler and grayer.

Charlie was keeping busy, too, starting new jobs and quitting them after he became bored. He worked in a windowless office that drove him crazy, at a Goodwill donation center where both the workers and donors were surprisingly rude, and at a school for delinquent boys where the rules he was asked to enforce seemed too cruel. "At every door, they have to ask, 'May I please pass through the threshold?' I wanted to tell them that in the real world, no one talks like that," he said.

He finally found a job in the university's mailroom, driving a van and delivering big boxes of mail to different buildings on campus. I think he liked it because he was in perpetual motion all day, seeing the town and getting outside in the fresh air. He also liked his co-workers, who were mostly macho Romanian guys who told him dirty jokes and taught him how to swear in their language.

By January, I was getting used to teaching and being a student again. I signed up to teach early morning classes in the spring semester just to get that part of my day done, hopefully leaving room to concentrate on my writing. I showed the same energy and enthusiasm during these early classes as I did for the afternoon ones in the fall, but this time my freshmen were even less amused. They sat at their hardwood desks and fell asleep in the crooks of their elbows. I hadn't taken into account how they would fare with the dark winter mornings in Iowa. Though I was getting used to it, I realized that my students had trouble waking up, let alone functioning coherently, in the bleakness of the morning.

I hadn't noticed such desolation myself until one day in late January. I stood at the bus stop in front of our apartment at 8:00 in the morning. It seemed like I was the only person awake, and I took advantage of the quiet to review the lecture I was about to give. I stood on the snowy sidewalk reciting my key points when I felt all the muscles in my body tighten. I rolled my neck and took a long breath of cold air through the thick wool of my scarf. I shivered from the weird sensation and tried to shake it off. At first, I blamed it on the weather.

The lawns and the roofs of the houses were covered with white. Snow moved in thin gauzy sheets across the road. The wind kept trying to push me off the sidewalk and onto the street, but I dug the heavy black soles of my boots into the snow. I was mummified, wrapped tight under layers of thermal underwear, fleece, and corduroy and nearly suffocating in a parka, scarf, and knit cap. If there was one thing I learned in Iowa, it was that you could never wear enough layers and that those layers couldn't be thick enough. And yet, six layers deep, it still felt like the cold air passed through me as if I were a sieve. Then, *oh no*, I thought, suddenly feeling as if the molecules I was composed of were breaking apart. I didn't know if the feeling was running through my blood or if it came from my gut or if it was me trying to doom myself with a bleak prophesy, but I just knew, standing there at that moment, that something was wrong with my kidney.

I'd seen this day coming across the horizon for a few years now, and I'd been given fair warning by the doctors that a transplant wasn't a cure for kidney disease, just another treatment. The original disease could come back in the transplanted kidney, or my body could start to reject it. Or it could just stop working, like a heart tired with age.

I knew what had to be done now. I had to call the nephrologist, who would probably order some blood work and maybe a biopsy of the kidney. Seeing as how I was now fresh out of siblings, I just hoped that the kidney would last me through to the summer, until the school year was over and I could better focus on the problem. I looked down the snow-covered road, and all I could see was a succession of tests, appointments, prognoses, and diagnoses, and as I had done for the cold Iowa winter, I braced myself for it.

THE NEPHROLOGIST I'D BEEN SEEING SINCE WE'D MOVED TO IOWA was a mouse of a woman with grayish brown hair and a nose that was too small for her face. She kept a close eye on me all fall because I was a new patient, not necessarily because she saw the rejection coming.

"That's what it is, right? Chronic rejection?" I asked her as we sat on the couch in her office. She brushed her hand against my back and confirmed my self-diagnosis. "We should start thinking about dialysis," she said.

"But, wait, it's not that bad yet, is it?" I had a feeling that the kidney was changing, but I hadn't recognized any symptoms yet.

No swollen ankles, no remarkable fatigue. Even my blood pressure was holding steady. I had called this one on a hunch, nothing more. I was just grasping the concept of actually being right; I didn't want to talk about what was going to happen next.

"Your kidney function is at about 50 percent now, but it's not getting any better. We can hold off putting a dialysis fistula in your arm for now. But that'll probably need to happen soon. I know you want to finish out the semester before you start any treatments, but I can't make that call right now. I suppose we can hold off and just watch your creatinine level every week," she said reluctantly.

I TRUDGED THROUGH WINTER IN A DAZE, TRYING TO STAY AHEAD of the schoolwork and the teaching just in case something were to happen. I should have been excited that my freshmen were finally looking more alive in class as the mornings became warmer, but no matter how well things were going in school or how much closer spring was getting, it always felt like I was still under the cloud of winter. After teaching my Monday morning class, I took the bus from the university to the hospital and had my blood drawn per Dr. Mousy's orders. I again put off her recommendation to have the surgery that would enlarge the vein in my arm—a procedure that would allow me to start dialysis treatment immediately after my kidney officially failed. I couldn't take a week off to recover from surgery right when my students were finally paying attention.

"Not yet, please," I begged her. "The semester is almost over."

One day, I sat in the kitchen of Beth's tiny bungalow staring at a shadowbox that held her collection of miniature things: a tiny hairbrush, a tiny glass pitcher, a tiny red harmonica. She was making a spinach cream sauce and stirring the pasta in a giant pot over the stove. "Should we have bread, too?" she asked me.

When I stood up to get a baguette from the counter, I caught a glimpse out the window. It was late spring, and Beth's backyard was getting into shape. She'd planted yellow flowers that now blossomed and curled along the edge of the yard; an overgrown tree that seemed menacing all winter was now trimmed and handsome. She had hosed down the white-painted iron patio table and chairs so they were free of leaves and dirt. Summer was going to be beautiful for her: quiet barbeques in the back, Saturday mornings tending to her new vegetable garden. I wondered what summer would look like for me. I didn't know if I'd be right there with her, or if I'd be in a hospital room trying to get better. I wanted to feel as hopeful as that bright backyard, but I had no clear window into my summer.

I must have been staring at the garden for a while because I heard her call, "Hello? Hello?" She grabbed the baguette from my hands and put it on the table. She looked at me through her black-rimmed glasses and said, "Clearly, you need a distraction. And so do I."

BETH WAS IN FINE PHYSICAL HEALTH, BUT HER LOVE LIFE WAS currently requiring her attention. She knew it, too, and she was trying to be cautious with her steps. She was a recent divorcée, ending her first marriage right after coming to Iowa. This was a fact that she didn't share with me until several months into our friendship, and even then, I had to grill her for details.

"I was too ambivalent," she'd said once, shrugging ambivalently.

"What does that mean?" I asked her. "Isn't the whole idea of marriage that you're making a choice? You pick someone and promise that you're going to be with that person for the rest of your life?"

"Yeah, I guess," she said. "We were dating, and everything was fine. And when he wanted to move here from Chicago, I told him I'd go. When he asked me to marry him before we left, I just sort of went along with it."

"I guess you didn't want him bad enough to try to work it out."

"I don't know. There's a point in a marriage when you can't go back to the beginning."

It had seemed she was ready to be single for a long while, not really mentioning anyone she was interested in and not really making an effort to meet anyone new. But then I'd heard reports that she and a professor from the media department were seen talking extensively with each other at two different parties.

"Beth," our friend Erica said at one of our many department potlucks, "you were spotted in a red car with a man." Everyone in the room turned to listen to her response, but Beth didn't make a peep. She sat in the corner rocking chair and stuck her nose deep into her wine glass, her cheeks visibly turning warm.

THE DISTRACTION BETH WAS REFERRING TO IN HER KITCHEN THAT afternoon turned out to be a job. At the Johnson County Administrative Building as a part-time transcriber. After working for a few days, she reeled me in, too.

It was the end of the semester by then, and after I had turned in my final grades, I knew I didn't want to sit at home and worry about what the rest of the summer would look like or when the kidney would shut down for good. So, for the early part of the summer, Beth and I sat in the air-conditioned office and listened to recordings of the daily county council meetings through headphones. There were months' worth of tapes that needed to be transcribed just to get up to date, so the work seemed endless. But I didn't mind the rhythm of it. It was a lot like what I imagined sewing to be, using the foot pedal to start and stop the tape, and hunching over the keyboard to watch my busy fingers at work.

Charlie liked that I was keeping busy, but wanted to make sure I was getting some rest, too. He'd call me a few times a day just to check that I wasn't wearing myself out. When I came home, I busied myself by reading or cooking, trying not to dwell on worst-case scenarios.

"I don't think you should stress out about the kidney, but I also don't think you should pretend like nothing's wrong," he kept telling me when I got quiet at night.

The kidney was holding on, as I hoped it would, but it was slowly starting to show signs that it was breaking down. I woke up one morning to find my mouth full of sores. The nurse at Dr. Mousy's office said it was a sign of end-stage kidney failure. I didn't talk for a week, and sadly, Charlie didn't seem to mind.

"This is what it takes for a man to get some peace?" he joked, poking my ribs so I'd at least smile.

Then at work one day, I hobbled like an old woman from my desk to the filing cabinet on the other side of the room. Beth caught me.

"What's wrong with you?" she asked.

"I don't know. I don't remember stubbing my foot or anything, but I woke up this morning and I couldn't step down on my big toe."

Later, when I wobbled off the sidewalk in front of our house and landed awkwardly on my ankle, Charlie took me to the emergency room. The doctor who tended to me said it was the gout.

"Huh?" I said. "Don't old people get that?"

"Usually," he said, looking at my chart, "but it's also a problem for people with failing kidneys."

Dr. Mousy was losing patience with me. At my next appointment, she tightened her lip and said, "I think it's time to get you some treatment."

"Just a little bit longer," I pleaded. I didn't know what I was waiting for. I guess I was just hoping that the future I hadn't planned for would finally sit right with me.

Dr. Mousy nodded, but not in a particularly comforting way.

As soon as I got back to the office, Tammy, our blond, Nordic-looking supervisor who had been transcribing Johnson County Council tapes for years, called me into her office.

"Look," Tammy said, pointing with her portly fingers to the monitor on which she had pulled up my most recent transcription. "You keep putting words in where they don't belong. Listen to the tape and then read what you've written. Your job isn't to edit the words, it's to transcribe them."

The next day, I was taking my time with a recording, slowing the tape down and rewinding it more often than usual, when my cell phone vibrated in my pocket. It was the doctor telling me that my weekly blood test came back and that my creatinine level was 6.6. "It's time," she said. "I'm not asking you this time, I'm telling you. We're doing this now."

I hung up the phone and swallowed hard. Tammy was on the phone, interns were shoving metal file drawers shut, and someone at the front desk was ringing the bell for service. Beth tapped away at a computer, wearing those black, puffy, donut-shaped earphones. When I came to her desk, she pulled them down and away from her face. "They're putting me on dialysis. I have to go," I said.

Beth, who usually hides her brown eyes behind her black-rimmed glasses, lowered her chin, looked at me over the frames, and bit her lip. "Oh, man."

"I have to go to the hospital. I have to tell Tammy what's happening. I have to call Charlie. Oh no, how is Charlie going to get to the hospital? What if—"

She stood up and seemed strikingly tall, especially when she put her hand on my shoulder to stop my breathless rant. "I will tell Tammy. I will call Charlie; I'll pick him up myself if I have to. You, go!"

I sat in the car in the office parking lot and breathed into the steering wheel. Then, I drove. I drove down a street called Summit, though there was no summit at all. Just a long, hot road that led to the hospital—an immense brick building that slowly began to fill my windshield as I neared it.

My kidney was no longer working, which meant that it could no longer regulate my blood pressure and clean my blood of toxins and waste. Eventually, I'd stop urinating, which meant my body was starting to hold on to liquid—swelling first my ankles and my hands, and then eventually flooding my whole body. My kidney had been working twenty-four hours a day to clean my blood, and now that it couldn't do that, I needed a machine to do that work for me. That treatment was called dialysis, during which long tubes would pull the blood from me, run it through the machine to clean it, and drain it back into my veins.

The problem now was how to get to my blood. Dr. Mousy had

wanted me to get the fistula in my arm for weeks now. The surgery of fusing together a vein and an artery of my arm together to make one big superhighway for the big dialysis needles was not an immediate solution. The new vein needed time to heal and grow. But since I needed a dialysis treatment right away, I had to get temporary access through a vein in my neck, or a catheter, which needed to be surgically inserted.

A nurse had me lie on a table in a procedure room and began cleaning off my neck with Betadine swabs. Dr. Mousy stood over me, too, claiming that this was a minor procedure and that I wouldn't feel anything. I kept my face tight and still as I looked up at her, telling myself that this was nothing. But soon my face was covered by a paper sheet and there was tightening in my neck. A surgeon who I couldn't see pulled and tugged at my skin as he twisted and turned a tube through my jugular. Before I knew it, I was taking shallow breaths and feeling the tears stream down my face, not really knowing if I was crying from the pain or from the fact that I was actually going through this, that this was happening.

"Over!" Dr. Mousy finally yelled. "See?" She pulled the sheet from over my face. "Rest here for a while. Let me talk with the nurses about when we'll get you on the machine." I heard her clogs as she stomped out of the room. I opened my eyes to see sinks and cabinets far off to the left and pale green tiles that worked their way up from the floor and onto the walls. I couldn't yet turn my neck to the right because of the pain and the bulkiness of my new appendage, but I could tell that I was on a very small table in a very big room. And I felt so lonely.

Dr. Mousy came in again to tell me they'd call me in soon. "And Charlie's here," she said. He stood behind her, leaning against the doorjamb, the sleeves of his chambray button-down folded up to his elbows. "We'll start the dialysis in a few minutes. For now, I'll leave you two alone."

Charlie leaned over me and pushed away a teardrop on my cheek with his thumb. "Why are you crying?" he said, though he knew the answer. His voice was quieter than I've ever heard it before. "There's no reason to cry."

He helped me up from the gurney, putting his hand between my shoulder blades as I sat up. The catheter swung like a pendant jutting from the side of my neck with tubes hanging from it. We walked in slow motion across the hall to a room as wide and as bright as a cafeteria, but free of tables and commotion. There were just white vinyl seats around a large nurses' station. Each of the seats had a machine beside it.

A nurse with blond hair and thick black roots walked us through the treatment procedure, showing us the scale where I would weigh myself upon entry and departure, showing us my assigned seat and machine. "There are blankets if you get cold. You'll probably get cold," she said. "Pillows, too, if you need them."

Once in the chair, I watched as she flushed my new catheter with a syringe of saline. Then she took the short tubes hanging from it and attached them to the long tubes dangling from the machine. There were buttons she pushed and liquid solutions she shook, but by the end of all her maneuvering, the long clear tubes that tethered me to the machine turned red with blood. I had started my treatment. "We'll just do a couple hours on the first day, okay?" she said. "Just holler if you need me."

Charlie sat in front of me on a stool, reading the digital numbers on the dialysis machine. He was scrunching his eyes over me to see, and then he focused back on me. "See, not so bad," he said. "There are some good parts to all this."

"Like what?" I said, my voice sounding a little hoarse.

"Well, it seems that dialysis has nothing at all to do with dying. It's a misnomer: *die*-alysis. Should be *live*-alysis."

"Thank god for misnomers," I said, smirking.

"Really!" he agreed. "This is going to make you feel better. For the past few weeks, I've been worried about getting a call that you were passed out on the floor or in an ambulance on the way to the hospital. But now, you're not going to get sick anymore. Now your blood pressure will even out and you'll quit getting those weird old lady problems."

"You don't even know what this is, Charlie. This is bad. Three hours a day, three times a week." I opened my hand and looked around the room. "This is like my second home now. It's like my new life." I heard the whining in my voice and I tried to trap the sound back into my mouth.

"Three hours? Do you know what this is? That's a nap! That's a long lunch! That's a couple soap operas and a talk show. Shoot, Moony, it's nothing."

The windows in the dialysis room were black now. It was past seven at night, and I realized that I was tired. The overhead light had been dimmed so the late-night customers could sleep.

"Have you eaten anything yet?" Charlie said.

"Not since lunch."

Charlie stood and asked a nurse who was passing by, "Can she eat?"

"Yes, something small," she said. "Something from the vending machines maybe?"

"Ah! She loves the vending machines." Charlie grinned in my direction. "What do you want?"

I pretended like I was trying to think about it. "I want Cheetos."

"You got it!" He stepped from the dimness of my room to the glow of the hall. My machine started a high-pitched beep just as Charlie faded out of sight. Immediately, the nurse with the black roots jogged from behind the nurses' station and headed toward me. She was not even done fidgeting with my machine before another one across the room began to beep.

"I swear these machines can talk to each other. They try to see how crazy they can drive me," she said. She was definitely younger than I was, maybe just out of nursing school, but she seemed like a veteran. She pressed a few buttons on the machine and swiftly poured liquid from one bottle into another, as if she were making a cocktail. She set the bottles down at the bottom of my machine, adjusted some tubes, then popped up on her white sneakers and headed toward the other noisemaker. "You should be fine, sweetie," she called back to me before she turned completely. "Just a little adjustment."

I didn't know what she had done, but now I was supposedly back on track—in a matter of speaking. But, really, there was more recalibrating to do. What now? Is teaching out? How was I supposed to plan for the summer, let alone the semester? This changed everything.

My co-patients in the dialysis room were few at this time of night. Later, I would learn that the prime-time slots were in the morning—best to get the burden out of your way as early in the day as you can. The few who were there were much older than I—a couple of grandmothers, a droopy old man whom I had yet to see open his eyes or lift his head. These were retirees with time to spare. In a secluded corner of the big room, behind a glass wall, there was one young man who seemed more muscular and fit than the others. He wore an orange jumpsuit and shackles around his ankles. He had his own private escort—a police officer—and they sat in the corner and watched TV. The irony of this man's situation was not lost on me: he was not only imprisoned by the state, but he was also shackled down to this machine. But as he and the police officer laughed in unison at whatever show they were watching, it seemed to me that the inmate wasn't really bothered by his situation.

When Charlie came back, I told him I wished this machine were draining more than my toxins away. I wished it were pulling this disease away, or pulling away everything that's wrong with my body. "You'd think that if they could come up with something to clean out your blood, they could figure out a way to get rid of the underlying problem, too," I told him.

Charlie put a hand down on each armrest of my chair and bent down so his eyes were even with mine: "Then pretend it does. This is a new moment for you. This is the new you. Pretend for a second that everything you're scared of is getting washed out by this machine. That somehow, you'll come out of this whole thing feeling refreshed and brand new. *Healthy*. Maybe even better than before."

"Yeah, right?" I said, exhaling with force.

"Really," Charlie said, not taking his eyes off mine. "Believe."

When I secured a morning time slot the following week, Charlie drove me to dialysis on his way to work. Sometimes Beth picked me up when I was through, or Bonnie, or whichever one of our friends was available. Sometimes I'd stand out on the sidewalk behind the hospital in the hot sun, weary and ready to pass out, and I'd wait for the campus bus to take me back home.

I quit my job at the Johnson County Administrative Building. Tammy didn't like me anyway. And I, apparently, was too distracted to pick up another distraction. On the days I had dialysis, I came home from the treatment and I slunk myself down on the couch. Charlie kept all the windows open all day to make sure I could smell the grass and watch the kids across the street blasting through the slip-n-slide. It was, after all, summer.

AFTER A FEW WEEKS OF COMING HOME TO FIND ME EXHAUSTED on the couch, Charlie came into the kitchen one day and offered me his kidney.

I was standing over the pea-green linoleum counter chopping onions to add to the stir-fry, so my eyes were already a little misty when he said, "I'll give you mine." He sat down in front of the kitchen table, laid his forearms in front of him, and entwined his fingers. I joined him, and a low-hanging pendant lamp lit the space between us and made me feel like we were in the interview room on a TV cop show. A comedy wherein investigators in shiny black suits hunched over us. I pursed my lips and waited for the punch line.

"It makes sense," Charlie said. "I'm here, I'm healthy, and it would take you off dialysis."

The options I had been presented with were clear: I could be put on the transplant waiting list. My father was thinking about donating, but I discouraged him, because I knew it would drive him crazy to be away from his patients for that long. I also did not want to imagine what kind of patient he would be. And my mother, though she was out of consideration because of her hypertension, offered to call in some favors to see if she could get a kidney off the black market. "Those people *want* to give their kidneys up," she reassured me when I brought up the ethics of selling and buying body parts.

But Charlie? The thought might have crossed my mind for a second, but the idea seemed like a stretch. First, he would have to want to do it. And he'd have to be a match. I couldn't stop thinking about what this would say about me. What kind of person asks her boyfriend for a kidney? I had dismissed the idea almost as quickly as I thought of it, and I had never mentioned it to Charlie.

It was hard for me to believe that now, as he was broaching the subject, I was slowly getting excited by the prospect of getting Charlie's kidney. But I tried to play it cool.

"We've got to get tested. And if you happen to match up, I'll give it some thought."

"Don't worry," he said, "we're a match." He nodded once, as if he knew it to be true. That's when a girl can start fantasizing and get her hopes up high. When she can stare across a table and see a pale white guy with a five o'clock shadow and a torn old T-shirt and see her Prince Charming.

"There are stipulations, of course," he said, squaring his shoulders.

"Of course," I said. I was just waiting for them.

"You've got to watch your diet."

I nodded enthusiastically.

"If we decide to do this, you've got to cut out the bacon, the Cheetos, and watch your salt intake. We'll keep an eye on your blood pressure." Our dietary habits in recent years had been a point of contention for me and Charlie, seeing as how Charlie had not only the mannerisms and humor of an old man but also the diet of one. Charlie was big on fiber, on an apple a day. On top of that, he was slowly eating less and less meat. Bad news for an omnivore girlfriend who was the main cook of the household. "Chicken, too?" I asked him.

"Chicken, especially!" Charlie said. "You know how they treat those birds? It's deplorable."

"But chicken is like 90 percent of my repertoire!" I protested. I couldn't imagine life without my mother's pork- and shrimp-stuffed *lumpia*, or her chicken *adobo*. And *lechon*. No roasted pig? Ever? I wasn't sure he was serious about his commitment until one night at a dinner party, when he'd waved off the hostess's flank steak and dove head first into the tofu meatballs.

The hostess had then turned to me and said, "You, too? Are you vegetarian?"

"No," I'd said, "I'm Filipino."

Back at the bargaining table, Charlie was waiting for a response. "Okay," I said. "A cleaner diet."

"No more drinking," Charlie continued. "I'm talking like one glass of wine at dinner, maybe. And no more smoking your 'occasional' cigarettes."

"Done," I said.

"And lots of exercise. You have to promise. I'm talking three days a week, half an hour of cardio. No more sitting on the couch. If I give you my kidney, you've got to keep it, be good to it. I'm not doing this for my health. I'm doing it for yours."

For me, I thought.

Charlie was concerned about his investment. And I couldn't blame him. He was hoping for a good turnout here; something that would last me a long time. But I wanted to make sure he was thinking about his side of the deal, too.

"There are factors you've got to think about."

"Like what?" he said.

"The surgery."

"No sweat. Slice me open," he said, running an imaginary scalpel across his midsection with his thumb.

"The tests—MRIs, x-rays, all that poking and prodding," I reminded him.

"I've gone through worse. Especially during those drug-testing years," Charlie reflected fondly.

"Rejection." This is the one that worried me the most.

"Moonface, come on, seriously. Could you ever reject this guy?" He pointed his thumbs in the direction of his chest. His eyes twinkled under the pendant light.

How could I? How could I ever reject him now? There was nothing about Charlie I could resist. In fact, I wanted to take all of him, not just his kidney. I wanted us to be like one person, one brain and one body, moving through the world. It was already starting to feel this way. I had already felt myself relying on him to verify my own feelings and to finish my half-baked ideas. Would taking his kidney make our relationship stronger? Would our plan even work?

"I don't know, Charlie," I said. "So many things have to go right."

"They will," he said, quick and sure. "Things will go right. Now, let's finish making dinner. I'm starving." He jumped out of his seat and walked toward the counter. The sun was setting in the window over the sink, and it outlined the power lines above our neighbor's garage. Shades of pink and lavender filled the sky. "Come on, Moonface," Charlie said, motioning to me with the knife. "Soak the noodles." I wanted to get up and help him, but I couldn't move. I was taking in this scene in the kitchen, which was well-lit even though daylight outside was slowly creeping away from us. Charlie chopped away at the cutting board, moving the knife in a wavelike motion over the onions. He lifted the slices from the board and heaped them onto a plate. He repeated this several times—chopping, then lifting, then stacking. He piled the stacks higher and higher until they were towering, precarious mounds. I sat in my seat, hoping they wouldn't fall.

Chapter Six

In an ACT of BRAVE STUPIDITY, TWO DAREDEVILS LAUGH in the FACE of DEATH

• • •

THE FIRST TIME I EVER SAW CHARLIE CRY WAS IN HAWAII. We had just started dating and were living in an expansive apartment overlooking Baker Beach in San Francisco with three dogs and six other humans. The real estate was prime, but it was difficult to have a romantic dinner without a tail wagging in your face or a hand trying to mooch off your plate. It wasn't the most ideal situation in which to start a relationship. Then, one day, Charlie goes: "Tell me where you want to go, Moonface. I'll take you anywhere."

"Hawaii!" I said, having never been and suspicious of his offer. But then Charlie started depositing fives or tens or anything he had into his bank account, and sooner or later, we were packing up our rucksacks and heading out over the ocean.

I woke up in the window seat on the plane and saw the entire island of Kauai from the air. A two-lane road wound around its circumference. Tiny cars drove between the ocean on one side and a dark, dense mountain that rose from the center of the island on the other. The ocean was sparkling, but I couldn't take my eyes off the mountain.

We weren't quite sure what we were doing there; we were both new to this. *What do people who are in love do?* Within a few days of our arrival, we found an apartment furnished with 1970s rattan chairs and a lumpy queen-size bed. It was on the southern end of the island, just a few yards from the beach. Charlie unpacked our rucksacks, stuffing our clothes into the closet shelves, and I walked down to the corner market to supply our kitchen with some basics.

At about four o'clock every afternoon, just as we got back from a swim, the sky would open up and a rain shower would move across the island, changing the mood from a balmy summer beach day to a cool, romantic evening. We left the windows in the bedroom open all day, and sometimes Charlie and I would make love to the sound of the rain on the palm trees and on the windows, before it quickly disappeared, and the quiet clear sky returned.

Our landlord, stopping me every time I walked past the rental office, gave me sugary-sweet oranges from the tree in his backyard. The neighbors, who were gone most of the day, were native Hawaiians who kept the place clean and quiet. I bought dishes and hand towels from the local Walmart, and with a few hundred dollars, we bought a well-used tan Oldsmobile from a guy who was sailing to Tahiti and selling everything he owned. The car had headlights that wouldn't turn off, so every time Charlie parked the car, he had to lift the hood and turn off the battery so it wouldn't drain. The owner threw in an electric typewriter with the deal for free.

"Why wouldn't you be totally happy in paradise? It's like you have no excuse," Charlie said, sipping a beer and leaning back on a lawn chair we found at the Goodwill.

In the tan clunker, we drove around the island looking for work at upscale hotels. We applied for every position—waiter, bartender, security guard. But because the island was so small, our prospects were low. We handed our resumes to everyone from Poipu Beach all the way up to Princeville. Nothing. We drove around the island, trying to keep a lookout for more prospective stores and restaurants. But my eyes kept being drawn to the middle of the island, to the dark, rainy spot at its center. The mountain, with its mossy flora and its ever-present rain cloud, seemed darker and creepier than it looked from the air.

We took a break from job hunting on Super Bowl Sunday to watch the Broncos play the Packers, in an open-air bar in walking distance from our apartment. I had many margaritas, as did Charlie, and we stumbled home, falling into the sand a few times and rolling over in laughter. The next morning, my head throbbing with a hangover, I started throwing up. This would be otherwise unremarkable except for the fact that once I started, I did not stop. Not that evening, not the next day, not the next evening. Charlie camped out beside me on the bathroom floor, but since he had yet to see me this sick, he really had no idea what to do.

"I'm just a puker," I tried to explain. This was true. At the first sign of illness, whether it was gastrointestinal or not, my body always tried first to get rid of whatever was in my stomach. I tried to convince him that it was probably something I had eaten, but by that third day, Charlie insisted on taking me to the emergency room.

"You're being ridiculous," he said as he pulled me off the bathroom floor and carried me to the car. In the outdated island hospital, with its walls of concrete blocks and its palm trees in the front lawn, we waited for hours for a general practitioner to review my blood tests. I wrung my hands as we waited and cried into Charlie's shoulder in the exam room.

"I'm scared," I confessed. "What if something is really wrong?"

Charlie was quiet and bounced his knee on the ground. He said he hadn't been in many emergency rooms and just didn't like the idea of hospitals.

The doctor who examined me deemed me officially dehydrated and not, in his opinion, having a problem with my kidney . . . yet.

"But if you plan on moving here, you should know that there are no nephrologists on the island. You'd have to fly to Oahu just to see a specialist. Just something to think about," he said, as he left us in the room to think about our next move.

I came back to the apartment feeling like a surfer who had just been tossed by a wave. I sat on the bed while Charlie pushed my clothes back into my backpack. It was not an easy decision when we agreed that I should go back to San Francisco and see a kidney specialist as soon as possible. Charlie'd follow once he got us out of the lease and sold the car.

"Geez, you're in it now," I told Charlie, as I watched him from the bed.

"Eh," Charlie said, "I don't know about the humidity here. And the sun! What's an Irish guy doing trying to get a tan? Our plan was just bound to fail."

I thought to myself that this was not the way to start a relationship. I didn't want to scare him off; I wanted him to find paradise with me.

He smiled at me as he moved from room to room gathering our things and putting them back in our bags. I lay on the bed and watched the walls turn dim. The sound of the rain rattled on the roof and it tapped metallically on the windowsills. I got up from the bed to find Charlie in the living room standing in front of the window, his chin to his chest, his shoulders rising and falling with his rapid breath, tears sliding down his face like raindrops.

HE COULD HAVE LEFT THEN. HE COULD HAVE SENT ME ON THAT plane and never followed me to San Francisco. But instead he flew to the mainland a few days later and took me to my doctor to make sure my kidney was still healthy, that it really was just dehydration. I had made him relinquish paradise, and brought him back to the rainy season in San Francisco, where the sun didn't burst through until March. So, years later, when Charlie offered his kidney to me, I joked to myself, *How much more does this guy have to give?*

NOT LONG AFTER CHARLIE MADE THAT OFFER, KERRY STOOD IN front of The Pita Pit waiting for me. Her corn-silk hair caught the bright sun even as she tried to hide under the awning. A red skirt partly covered her long heron legs. Kerry was another writer in my program who came to Iowa the year before I did. She brought her Long Island wit with her, but seemed softer and gentler than most New Yorkers I knew. She wrote often about death, about her mother dying from melanoma when Kerry was still young. But for someone who thought about death as much as she did, she was lively and joyous whenever I saw her. She celebrated everything. I liked her from the moment I met her, but didn't always like her hugs, because they were like choke holds around my chest. Her bony arms were deceiving. I wove through a crowd of college students on the sidewalk to finally get to her, and when I did, she grabbed me tightly and nearly collapsed both my lungs, as usual.

"How are you feeling?" she said. I hadn't seen Kerry since the end of the semester, but I assumed she'd heard of my recent medical dilemma. I had heard she was taking the summer easy, jogging in the morning and writing in her attic apartment in the afternoons. When she had called a few days before, she was eager to meet. It was only after we found a table that she came clean. "I don't really want a pita," she said.

"I think they have other things," I said, scanning the paper menu. "Subs, salads."

"I want to give you my kidney," she said.

I looked up, and the collar of her jean jacket was brushing against her glossy pink lips. Her face was frozen with a raised eyebrow waiting for me to answer.

"Pardon?" I said. The place was loud; surely I had heard her wrong.

"I want to give you my kidney."

"What could possibly possess you to do a thing like that?" Behind her was a wall mural of a giant dancing pepper, and as I slid back in my red plastic chair, I tried to negotiate the seriousness in her face with the goofiness of that pepper. There was an eggplant, too, which was not helping.

"I want to help. My mother always told us that if you *can* help, then you *should*. This, I can do."

"No way," I said almost instinctually, shaking my head, thinking that this *was* as silly as a dancing eggplant. She didn't know what she was getting into. I knew she wanted to help me, but this was not going to be the way she was going to do it.

"Look," she said, leaning into toward the table and softening the lines in her face, "I want you to know that I've thought about it and I want to donate it to you. I want to at least get tested."

Her voice dropped low, and I could tell that she had thought it through, that this was something she had already committed herself to before coming here. Knowing this, my heart swelled. I could feel it filling my chest, pushing against my sternum, making it hard to breathe. This girl just loved to take my breath away. I went over my relationship with Kerry in my head. I had known her for less than a year. Even though I barely saw her during the week, when we would sit down to chat at a park bench, our talks lasted for hours, long after the school kids threw their backpacks on the ground, goofed around on the jungle gym, and went home. Why would she give her kidney to me? I almost didn't want to tell her that I would be taking Charlie's donation. But when I did, she let me know that the offer would stand: "In case, you know, something doesn't work out."

Later that week, my mother, who had begun reporting on my health to everyone she knew, told me that my cousin Joanne in California had called. She wanted to give me her kidney, or at least get tested, too.

"So sweet," I told my mother, but to myself, I thought: *What is wrong with these people?* This was major surgery they were committing to, opening their bodies and letting me steal a living part of them. I would not accept their offers, but would it be wrong of me to keep them on reserve, in case, you know, things actually didn't work out?

"That's impossible," Charlie said when I confessed this to him. He folded his arms over his chest and said, "You don't need a backup."

Our transplant coordinator at the hospital agreed with him. The medical team had already begun the poking and prodding process to see if he would be a fit. Charlie came home from the clinic, happy to show me the papers on which it was repeatedly stated that none of Charlie's results came back abnormal.

"Healthy as a horse," he told me. "Someone actually used the cliché."

I watched our coordinator's pink lipstick as she sat across the conference table and said, "He's good enough."

"Perfect, you mean," Charlie corrected.

"Well, your blood type is O-, so you are a universal donor. That works out great. But your antigens—it's impossible that the two of you would match all six. You matched one. We were hoping for more, but one will work."

"So he'll work?" I asked her.

"Told you," Charlie said, smiling annoyingly. I just knew it was coming.

CHARLIE'S MOTHER CALLED ONE EVENING IN LATE MAY. SHE called often to check on us in those days, when my health was slowly fading. Charlie talked to her on the phone in the kitchen, and I listened from the living room as their normally uneventful weekly exchanges suddenly became heated.

"No, she's fine, she's lying on the couch."

"I won't . . . No . . . What? . . . No, mom, we've got it covered . . . No!"

His voice grew louder but not in the usual excited, sprite way Charlie turns up the volume. He stood up from the wooden chair and paced the floor in short, impatient laps. When I sat up from the couch, he looked at me, and shaking his head, he mouthed: "She wants to give you her kidney."

It was her insistence that was driving him mad, that she wasn't listening to him when he told her that he wanted to do this, that he *had* to this. I watched Charlie from the edge of my seat on the couch as if he were in a boxing match. I wanted to throw my hands in the air and say "Move to the left" and "Don't forget the ropes!"

"Mom, we'll be fine." He sat down again, putting his elbow on the table and his head in his hand. "You're not doing this . . . No."

CHARLIE'S MOTHER HAD ALWAYS BEEN SOFT-SPOKEN AND EVEN-tempered, quietly listening as we told her where we were moving to next. She didn't yell at Charlie when he took long hiatuses from working. Instead she'd bring up the subject of money and careers to him slowly, over dessert, in quiet conversations that lingered nowhere near the topic. But once she started, she didn't stop. She wanted him to know that there were other things he could do with his life.

"Physical therapy," she would say to him repeatedly. "You're very athletic, you know. Or a teacher. You love kids!"

Charlie would always kindly turn down her suggestions, and then grab my leg under the table in frustration. She welcomed me into her home and into their lives and always treated me like the daughter she had always longed for. I liked the times when she and I stood in the kitchen over a cup of tea, and she'd tell me stories about Charlie's childhood: his boundless energy that she had given up trying to contain, his friendship with his stuffed penguin, his imaginary friends.

This time, it was clear that she was trying to protect Charlie. I remember Charlie telling me that she had lost her own mother at a young age because of complications from a routine surgery. I understood where she was coming from, and I was overwhelmed that yet another person was willing to put her life on the line for me.

But, honestly, at that moment, I wanted her to stop talking. "This is ours," I wanted Charlie to say. "Ours." This transplant was something that Charlie and I were meant to do together, and I didn't want her to come between that. I wanted to think he was thinking the same thing as his voice rose higher into the receiver. His blue eyes bulged with the frustration he was keeping in. He held firmly to the phone, his knuckles stretched tightly over the receiver.

It was only when he made an excuse that she couldn't factually dispute that she backed off: "Think about it, Mom. I think it would just be better for her to have a twenty-eight-year-old kidney than a fifty-year-old one."

As I heard him fighting for the right to do this, fighting for us, I thought that this was bigger than an operation. When he finally got off the phone with her, he shook his head, and ran his hands through his hair, looking like he'd just come out of a knock-down, drag-out fight.

This was our story. From the moment he spoke of it, I dreamt that our connection was exclusive. In order for Charlie to live and function as part of my body, I had to believe that this was more than the simple swapping of serum, or organs changing places, or the rewiring of equipment. I had to believe that with kidney transplants some sort of magic exists.

Consider the evidence: Six months after my first transplant, my mother sat in my aunt's kitchen and spoke to her in Tagalog. I noticed how her voice lowered when I walked into the room.

"She's different, you know," she whispered to Aunt Bella.

I was passing through the kitchen, taking a break from the

movie my cousins and I were watching in the next room. I stood over the sink and reached up to the cupboards for a glass.

"She's feeling better?" my aunt asked, looking at my mother over the lenses of her reading glasses.

"Mmm . . . yes," my mother said, "but she's different." She leaned in close, whispered to her. "She's just like her brother."

I stopped pouring and listened closely from around the corner. "She quickly gets angry now. Short temper. She's a *bruja*."

"Mom! Quit it!" I snapped.

"See?" She raised her eyebrows and looked at my aunt, avoiding my glare.

My mother had taught me Tagalog when I was growing up, naming the words for things I pointed to in both ways—in both English and in Tagalog. But I didn't need to be skilled in either of those languages to know from her tone and her facial expression that *bruja* meant "witch."

"I'm being honest, not mean," she said to me. "You get that way now. I think it's in the kidney." She was referring to my brother's quick temper. She always said that he was quick to laugh, but just as quick to anger. This was true; his fuse was short. But I certainly wouldn't call him a male witch.

For the longest time, I didn't believe her. But when I started feeling healthy and stronger, so unlike myself, able to run down the street, run like hell, with the energy and athleticism of my brother, I started to believe that something in me was changing. At a checkup after the surgery, I asked one of the surgeons quietly if my mother was onto something.

"I know I could take on his kidney's health, but could I take on his personality traits, too?"

"That kind of thinking can get you in trouble," the doctor said.

But, with Charlie, I felt in trouble *without* that kind of thinking. This exchange seemed too carnal—too scientific, too strictly biological—without the idea that Charlie and I could be connected on some other level. These weren't body parts that were made in labs or regenerated from orphan cells. These were living cells from living people. I had to believe that love could sweep in here, that there was a mystical factor involved in this exchange. That Charlie and I—not blood related, not even married—were going to be united by a greater force. Part of him would live in me, no matter what. I'd be with him. Forever.

AFTER LOSING MY BROTHER'S KIDNEY, I THOUGHT FOR MANY months that it might have been something I had done. *Was it my fault? Was I eating the wrong foods? Drinking too much beer? Was I not taking care of myself enough?*

"No, it's none of these," my brother said on the phone after he heard the news. "Ten years—we had a good run."

I joked with him, "Well, if you've got another to give, I'll take it."

He hung up the phone abruptly.

Charlie kept telling me not to think too much about that stuff. "It wasn't your fault at all. Sometimes things just happen. They make room for other things."

His mind was set that this was going to work, and I tried to follow his lead, but there always seemed to be something to worry about.

"What will Charlie's family think? They'll think we're not willing to help you, that we're relying on other people to help you," my mother told me once on the phone. At first, she didn't like the idea of Charlie's donation, her Filipino pride making her hesitant to receive help from outside the family.

"Well, his mother tried to take his place, but he wouldn't let her," I told her.

"Ay, *anak*," she said. "Look at all these strangers trying to help you."

"They're not strangers, Mom," I said. "They're like family."

"Well," she said, thinking about it, "yes, but not yet."

IN MIDSUMMER, I TOLD CHARLIE THAT THE DIALYSIS TREATMENTS were beginning to wear on me. My appetite was decreasing, and my broomstick arms were looking silly in tank tops. He could tell I was getting anxious, so he suggested that we take a quick trip back to Baltimore while the hospital finalized our surgery date. We wanted to see Charlie's newborn niece anyway—a nine-pounder who was quickly gaining more weight. "We have to see her before she weighs more than you," Charlie said. We rescheduled my dialysis treatments so they fit snuggly around a three-day weekend, and we took off due east.

I knew Charlie was excited to be back home, but I was a little worried about seeing his family and hearing what they had to say about him giving me his kidney. I knew they were jokesters, that the funny bone had passed down through the lineage, and that they protected members of their brood with their lives. If Charlie's mother wasn't enough evidence of that, take, if you will, my memory of meeting Charlie's dear Aunt Wendy for the first time. She had shaken my hand, and then put that same hand over Charlie's chest. "If you break his heart, I will hunt you down and I will hurt you," she'd said. At first, I was too scared to look at her. But when she got a riotous reaction from other family members who stood nearby, I knew she was using those words for comedic effect. Afterward, she slapped my shoulder and gave me a hug.

"Okay, I get it. Your family loves you," I'd said to Charlie. I had known how Charlie's family felt about his heart, but I was afraid to find out how they'd feel about me taking one of his other organs.

"Don't worry. You don't have to tell them," Charlie said. "I will. Just follow my lead. Trust me, they won't think you're an organ harvester."

"A kidney hog," I said.

"The Renal Reaper," Charlie said.

In the living room of Aunt Wendy's house, we walked into a boisterous welcome from aunts, uncles, and cousins waiting in line to bear-hug Charlie and gently wrap their arms around me.

"You look well," Aunt Wendy said to me, looking at my face carefully. I wanted to believe her, but I knew that I was tired from the flight and probably looked so. Charlie's grandmother stood behind me and brushed my hair with her fingers.

"Hi, Grandma!" I said, turning around.

"Look at that hair. Such beautiful black hair. Such pretty straight hair," she said. "Come look at this, Wimpy." She called Charlie's grandfather over, and Pop, the bounding octogenarian, came to give me a hug.

"Yeah. Pretty girl, ain't she? You still got that pretty hair, too, Holly. Feel it!" Pop put Grandma's shaky hand up to her head. Charlie's grandmother was older than Pop, and not quite as quick as he was anymore. I was happy she remembered me. I watched the two of them as they remembered what she looked like years ago, her hair curly and less gray. Pop eased his arm around her as he escorted her back to the couch, and I could see where Charlie got his charm.

Charlie and I lingered around the party separately, but I always kept one eye on his location, just in case someone were to ask me about the transplant. I wasn't sure how I'd respond; I was hoping that it wouldn't come up at all. I was hoping that we could explain our little exchange after it had happened, after both of us were in the clear. But it never came up, and I spent a large part of the afternoon holding Charlie's niece Genevieve, a soft, sleepy bundle impervious to Charlie's loud relatives. She burped in her sleep, wriggled in my hands, and tried to suck on the edge of my collar. She was the first thing that I'd held in a while that was warm and alive and full of life. I was staring at her tiny nose when I heard Charlie say, "I have an announcement!"

The whole room paused and focused on Charlie.

"You're getting married!" Aunt Dayle called out. There were audible gasps of excitement.

"No," Charlie said, bowing his head in shame. The crowd looked disappointed. I knew they would be. They had been asking us for years now when we were going to make it official. We'd always dodged the question in the past; I wondered how Charlie was going to dodge it this time. I handed off the baby to Charlie's mother and stood behind him at the front of the room. I wasn't going to let me him face the fire by himself.

"My lovely Moonface here is in need of a kidney." He grabbed my hand. "And I am her lucky donor."

The crowd fell silent. This time, they seemed confused. "Wait, what?" Charlie's uncle asked, seeming shocked by the news of my illness. "She needs a transplant?"

"Yes!" Charlie said, pulling me closer to him.

"And you said you'd do it?" his Aunt Wendy asked loudly, like he was out of his mind. "Why?"

"I heard there would be drugs," Charlie said, shrugging. His father cackled in the corner.

"Jean, what do you think of all this?" Pop asked. He and the rest of the room turned around to look at her.

"I think it's lovely. But I was hoping they'd be married by now," Charlie's mother responded from the couch, trying to talk over the baby who was now crying in her arms. "Then it would be more romantic, wouldn't it?"

Charlie looked confused. "What do the two have to do with each other?" he asked.

"It's just more of love story, isn't it?" Aunt Dawn asked, sticking with Jean.

"Wait, I have an idea," Charlie's father said, standing up to address the crowd. "This is actually the perfect opportunity for a wedding." He hunched over liked he was in a football huddle, and he was the one calling the play. His hands waved and directed how the action will go. "We wheel them in to the O.R., and once they're both unconscious, we bring a justice of the peace. He makes it official, and when they wake up, they'll be married, and transplanted. And none the wiser."

"Ugh," someone from the audience groaned, rejecting the bad joke.

"I wish I was being transplanted to India right now," I told everyone. There were a few giggles.

"Nah," Charlie said. "Family members arrange marriages there, too!" Someone laughed harder, and I could see the faces of shock turning into smiles.

"A priest!" Charlie's grandmother yelled. "No justice of the peace. A priest!"

"We could find him some black scrubs with a collar. We'd have to sterilize the Bible!" a cousin insisted.

"But who'll take the pictures? The nurses?" someone said.

"We'll have it videotaped."

"The wedding or the surgery?"

"Whichever is more interesting! Both! We'll keep both for posterity."

Charlie and I watched as the dialogue connected the dots across the room, each member of the family feeding off each other's twisted idea of a joke. Charlie put his hands on my neck and massaged my shoulders, forcing me now to relax and watch the show.

"See, Charlie, this would all be easier if you were married first. Then we wouldn't have to be worried about the surgery *and* your nuptials."

"All right, wait!" Charlie said, as loud as his voice could get. "The truth is, I did actually set a date for our wedding." His eyebrows looked serious. He put one hand to his side, picked up a beer, and looked into the glass. Everyone was hanging on, even the baby, who seemed to be holding her wailing until Charlie spoke again. I sat and waited to hear, too.

"June," he announced, pausing to build suspense, "of 2030!"

"Come on!" The frustrated crowd yelled. The aunts in the back by the kitchen laughed and threw their napkins in the air, but everyone grew silent when Charlie's sweet, frail grandmother stood up.

"But Charlie," she yelled, "I'll be dead by then!"

The mob roared.

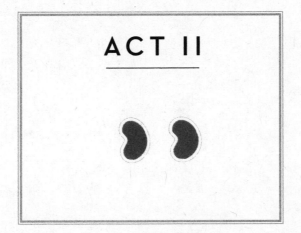

ACT II

Chapter Seven

The INQUISITOR, the PAIN INFLICTOR, and a SPECIAL GUEST APPEARANCE by the BLINDING TRUTH

. . .

WELL, THE TRANSPLANT WENT OFF WITHOUT A HITCH, AND without us getting hitched, the latter being much to everyone else's dismay. I got my plumbing rewired to fit Charlie's hardware, and Charlie got out of there with a hole in his gut. On the day of the surgery, there may have been more reasons to worry, like the danger I was putting Charlie in and if the kidney would actually work. But Charlie wouldn't even let it enter my mind. This time, when they lined my gurney in the hallway next to my donor's, there were no holy figure sightings. There was barely any fear in Charlie's face or tenderness in his eyes as they wheeled him toward the double doors of the O.R. As they pushed him through, he only shouted out one warning back at me: "Look out for priests!"

When I woke up, my folks stood over me and told me Charlie did fine, and that the first words out of his mouth were, "Is she peeing?" Before I could even crack a smile, Charlie walked through the door of my room, his left hand clutching the IV pole and his right arm draped over his father's shoulder.

"What took you so long, Moonface?" he bellowed. "I've been awake for hours!" He leaned down to kiss me with barely any effort at all.

Now, three weeks after the transplant, he still doesn't let anyone see the effects the nephrectomy has had on his body. "Nephrectomy, freschectomy," he scoffs, even though, every once in a while, I'll catch him jumping out of bed, then immediately regretting that he did so, holding his guts in place for a second before moving again.

"Quit showing off," I say.

"Don't want to disappoint the crowds," he says. Sad part is he's not kidding. We feel a little like celebrities now, keenly aware that our fame is spreading around town. An unending parade of visitors clues us in, streaming through the apartment delivering food and magazines and flowers. Our friend Maria had brought over a cardamom and cranberry pie. Beth called from clear across the country while taking a road trip with that media department professor she'd been seeing. The "Make It or Break It Trip," she'd called it, testing how long the two could endure each other's company. She felt guilty about not being here during the surgery, but I had told her that the surgeons hadn't been wondering why she didn't scrub in. Amy, another friend, had brought over a plant and watched quietly as we moved awkwardly around the furniture and as Charlie slipped out of character once and grimaced when he made room for me on the couch.

Our parents stuck around for two weeks after the transplant, waiting on us hand and foot so we barely had to move. But now that they're gone, I've noticed Charlie's quick rebound from surgery slowing down. His activity during the first few days in the hospital was boundless, but that was probably because the anesthesia was still pumping through his veins. Now the incision seems to bite at his side more frequently, no matter how much he tries not to show it.

After our parents leave, we venture out of the house for the first time down to another student's house for a potluck. Charlie pauses on the corner of College Avenue.

"Wait," he says, looking down at the ground.

"What? Did we walk too far?" I look up at him and try to gauge the expression on his face.

He holds his hand over the dressing of the wound and breathes slowly.

"It hurts, doesn't it?" I ask. "Oh crap oh crap oh crap. I knew we shouldn't have walked." I look around in case there's someone near to help.

"I just need a second," he says, and we sit on the sidewalk until the pain subsides.

I stare at him, my eyes squinting at the sun behind the trees. "You look like you're in pain, too," he says, laughing a little when he sees me.

"A little," I say.

"No, you're not," he says. "You're supposed to tell me that you're feeling better."

I would, but it seems too cruel to tell him so. Better to let him think we're suffering together.

• • • •

I tell Charlie we don't have to go to Erica's. "Let's keep going," he says. "We'll just walk slowly. You want to see everyone, don't you? Show off that new kidney of yours."

He knows I do. I've spent the summer hiding from everyone else in town, trying to shield myself from the sad, apologetic faces most people make when they see me paler and thinner than usual. I do want to show off my new self, but it's hard for me to imagine enjoying myself at a party when Charlie is curled up in a corner unable to move.

When we get to Erica's, a room full of writers with small paper plates and glasses of wine in their hands smile to greet us.

"You look completely revived," Beth says. She is tanned and aglow herself. I see the professor in the kitchen talking to someone near the fridge.

"How's Charlie?" she asks.

"Well . . ." I say, taking my time and trying to find a good answer. I don't know how to explain to her that while I might look like a hundred percent, I won't feel that way until Charlie is back to himself.

While I'm trying to think, Charlie jumps in and answers for me. "How do I look, Beth? Handsome as usual? Like I've dropped a pound or two around my hip region?"

"If that's what donating a kidney does to you, I might have to sign up," says Richard, a writer from Missouri. He told us from the start of the process that he has always been in awe of Charlie's "selflessness," making Charlie blush at the word.

"Donation? My arse! That femme fatale took it from me!" Charlie says, pointing an accusatory finger in my direction.

"What?" I say, playing along, but really unsure what he's getting at this time.

He goes on: "So one night, Moonface says to me, 'Charlie, let's have a romantic dinner.' And I say, 'Yes, darlin',' thinking any night's a good night to get lucky. She makes us a little pasta, pours us some wine, kisses my neck, and then after that, the whole thing gets a little hazy. The next thing I know I wake up, and I'm neck-deep in a bathtub full of ice. Pain is shooting through the left side of my body. Moonface is standing over me with a cleaver."

Some people chuckle at his outrageous yarn and at his theatrical performance.

"Correction!" I interrupt. "It was a paring knife. For precision."

"She took it from me! The heartless harpy took my kidney!"

"You weren't willing to give it to me, wimp. What was I gonna do? You didn't need it; you said you were willing to donate it."

"You misunderstood," he says calmly and clearly. "I said I would donate . . . money . . . to the National Kidney Foundation . . . in your honor."

The crowd is a chorus of giggles, many of the guests shaking their heads. They're too distracted to see Charlie walking backward and taking a seat on the couch, clinging to the armrest for support. No one notices but me.

I SHOULD START THINKING ABOUT MY CLASSES SOON, AS SEPTEMBER is just around the corner. I worried all summer long that the surgery would fall through, and so I haven't really prepared. I'm looking through my books at the kitchen table one day while Charlie's on the couch watching yet another episode of *Sesame Street*.

"Are you regressing?" I ask him.

"No. I'm bored. We don't have cable, and PBS is the only educational thing on," he says without taking his eyes off the TV.

I get up and sit next to him on the couch, and I squeeze him around his shoulders. I lean over to give him a kiss, and he holds out a cheek for me.

"You know, Charlie, I don't know why the heart is classically defined as the symbol of love. No way! I say the kidneys! You're born with two: one to keep and one to share. You can't literally give someone your heart. "

"Well, technically you can," he says.

"Yeah, but that's really not fun for everyone, is it?"

He grabs his cup from the table and stands up slowly to refill it. As he teeters toward the kitchen, I think, I'm not sure, but I think I hear him say, "But neither is this."

I FIND THAT WHEN PEOPLE ASK ME ABOUT THE TRANSPLANT, THEIR eyes well up in a corny kind of way that makes for some awkward silences as they try to look up to make their tears trickle back into their eye sockets. Or maybe it's awkward because I'm afraid I'll start to well up, too. Or that our corny love story feels like a farce, that maybe I really did take the kidney from him against his will and left him with the raw end of the deal.

Every time someone asks about us, I'm tempted to tell them Charlie's been on the couch for a few weeks now, that he stares out the window and looks the way I did all summer long while I was on dialysis.

It's not like he doesn't try, though. When the occasion calls, he can gather himself in new clothes and find his old spark again in a snap. Charlie realized at the first few parties after the surgery that it is easier for him to make startling proclamations than to try to explain how bad he really feels. Before a crowd of friends, Charlie explains that his kidney will not fail because it is half German.

"Half German?" I repeat for clarification.

"*Ja, frau!*" he says, standing straight and trying to hold his chest out in front of him like a male gorilla. "From the fair Kritvise side of the family."

Our friend Maria, surname of Stadtmueller, agrees. "*Ja!*" she says with conviction, her sunny, freckled face suddenly turning stern and decidedly Bavarian. We are sitting at a card table on Erica's front porch, and a streetlight is illuminating Maria's strawberry blond hair from behind.

"*Ja*, Marr-eee-ah" Charlie says, in his best Arnold Schwarzenegger impression. His voice drops low and his jaw overextends.

"Schwarzenegger was Austrian," a snarky voice from behind the screen door yells.

Charlie snaps back: "Same accent, though." He is annoyed by the details.

"Yeah, German kidney. So, what difference does it make?" I ask. Clearly there's something he's getting at here, and I want to help him get there.

"Discipline. It will become the master of all those other organs and keep them in order. *Achtung*, all you other organs!"

"*Achtung!*" The German Maria follows. She loves this.

"That sounds a little racist," Erica says.

"Why, because she is Asian? It's just that I have strong genes," Charlie says.

"That sounds worse," Erica says.

"But you're half Irish, too. Right?" I remind him.

"Hmm," Charlie says, pondering for a moment.

I find the perfect comedic timing and jump: "Let's just be glad you didn't give me your liver!"

We lift our wine glasses and toast to that.

In fact, there is no sign of my body rejecting Charlie's kidney. My weekly blood tests show only astounding numbers. And while I don't have reason for concern, I still wake up in the morning to assess my body—trying to see if I can feel a change, any change. Anything new. I look in the mirror and check out my face for any signs. I don't know what I'm looking for, but I keep an eye on it. Once, Charlie came into the bathroom and loosened the worried lines in my brow with his thumb. "Relax, Moonface."

"I should be worrying about you," I told him.

"Nah," he said. "You shouldn't be worrying about anything."

Later at the party, I escape into the corner of the room, watching people move between us in waves and overhearing conversations about us.

"But, if this is her second transplant, isn't that better?" Alice, an environmentalist and fellow student, asks, trying to sound hopeful.

Joan, the mathematician, says, "No, that makes no sense. Where did you hear that?"

"Yes," Charlie says, "better is second, I reckon."

Joan completely ignores Charlie's imaginative rhyme. "Absolutely no sense," she repeats. "That's completely unfounded."

Alice says, "No, I read it somewhere. Something about the antibodies or—"

"No, that's wrong. It's about the body's ability to tolerate the drugs," Richard tunes in. Soon the room is debating the likelihood of my new kidney's long-term survival. They go on, these experts, with an impromptu panel discussion about transplantation, while Charlie escapes from the middle of the porch, sneaks inside past the kitchen, slides in beside me, and whispers into my hair: "If they only knew that this kidney is going to outlive the both of us."

THE SECOND TIME I EVER SAW CHARLIE CRY WAS ON THE FLOOR of our bedroom.

Two days after the operation, Charlie was soft-shoeing down the hallway proving that his intestines were working by demonstrating to the doctors that he could pass gas (and providing them with way more evidence than they needed). So Charlie got to go home early while I stayed at the hospital. A day later, the doctors let me follow him, making sure we were going to be taken care of by our families. This sounded like a good idea at the time. Our parents were staying at our friend Bonnie's house a few streets away. But, by choice, they only used Bonnie's house for sleeping. They spent most of the day at our bedside monitoring our every move.

Charlie's problems after the surgery started with our mothers, whose constant doting was selfless and sweet, but for two weeks in a tiny underground apartment, often suffocating. Depending on them for everything was not unlike living at home all over again. Our first morning started out peacefully. Charlie and I woke up to the sun coming through the window.

"Not so bad," Charlie said, his eyes barely open, a deep exhalation to follow.

"No, not so bad at all," I said. "And I have to pee!"

"Pee! Pee! She's peeing! She's peeing!" Charlie said, acknowledging the triumph of a healthy kidney transplant.

But when I opened the door, the waft of coffee filled the room.

Charlie, who hates the smell of coffee, playfully gagged.

Over the next few days, our parents brewed coffee and spoke loudly outside our bedroom door, and though they wanted us to come out and join them, it was hard being with them sometimes, keeping up with my mother's boisterous laughter or their constant questions. Most of the time, we just wanted to sleep. We were still recuperating and none of our systems had yet gone back to normal. I woke up one night to find Charlie bent facedown over the floor, his rear sticking straight up in the air.

"Charlie!" I gasped.

"I'm fine. Go back to sleep."

The next morning, as we lay in bed reading, Charlie tore a piece of notebook paper out and gave it to me. On it was a cartoon of a skinny man with blue curly hair and a bloated stomach, and in that stomach, there was a TV, a telephone, a piece of furniture, a tree, an apple, a refrigerator, a bicycle, and some small birds. "That's how I feel right now," he said, before standing up slowly and trying one more time for the bathroom. We knew that one of the hardest parts of the surgery was getting his intestines back on task. Coupled with the painkillers, which slowed his system even more, he was in agony.

Though I felt like I could walk all over Iowa City, I tried to stay close to Charlie. But, that evening, our parents left, and I was putting things on the shelf, arranging books by author from A to Z, fiction and nonfiction, poetry and plays. All night Charlie had paced up and down the long hall. When I was done with my redecorating, I found Charlie curled up on the floor, his knees almost to his chin, crying over the cramped feeling inside him.

• • •

"LET'S TALK ABOUT THE PAIN," SHE SAYS. JOAN IS NOT A SADO-masochist. She just really wants to know. She might be a hypo-chondriac, but I'm not sure. Maybe she just complains a lot. But I think she just really wants to understand.

There's a bookstore with a coffee shop that Charlie and I fre-quent. Steam's always rising from people's coffee mugs as they type away on their laptops. Charlie and I come for tea and to browse the aisles, and there is always someone there we know. A woman I know greets me as I stand in line. She has a no-nonsense haircut kept high and tight. Sometimes, questions come out of her mouth before she considers what she's asking.

For example: the last time I saw her, I was in the middle of kidney failure, with all the symptoms emerging all over my body. Canker sores had taken over my mouth and I was trying to speak without them showing. I thought I was being discreet by putting a hand over my lips, but as I answered Joan's greeting, she had twisted her face and asked, "What's wrong with your mouth? Did you have dental work or something?"

Another time, Charlie saw her walking up the side of a coun-try road and pulled up beside her and asked if she wanted a ride. She looked inside the window at his exposed arm on the steering wheel, and the first words that came out of her mouth were, "Is that a rash?"

When we see her in line for her coffee, Charlie quickly ducks into the graphic-novel section deep in the store's interior. Sly fox. When we sit down at a table, she looks me straight in the eyes through her thick lenses, and I think I will try to squirm my way out of this. I try to be clear without lying.

"What were you feeling?" she asked.

"Well, obviously, the incision was sore."

"How about before then? Did your kidneys—or your kidney—

hurt? Did it feel like your kidney was trying to leap out of your body?" She grabs at the skin around her waist and squeezes. She scrunches her face; she furrows her brow. She looks like she's taking a poo.

"No, the kidney didn't hurt. I couldn't really feel that."

"Dialysis?"

"Yes, getting the dialysis catheter."

"Yes," she says, "tell me about that." I go through details with her, the slow insertion of the tube in my neck, how I felt like I was not human, but a robot with interchanging parts out for repair. I go on and on, making the stitches, the cuts, and blood-letting, skin-tearing details more scenes from a horror film than a medical procedure.

Her rapid-fire questions shoot holes in my brain. Little holes that open up spots I'm afraid will leak. I don't tell her about seeing Charlie writhing in pain, curled up like a child on the bedroom floor. I leave out the part about the tears I caused him, how those moments are ingrained in my memory like scars, and how I replay those scenes and look for ways to call them back and change them. No, I don't tell her about that pain.

AFTER THE TRANSPLANT, CHARLIE WENT TO HIS OWN CLINIC appointments, where the doctors checked to see if he was healing up nicely. He wasn't. An infection on his incision kept getting worse even though we thought it was getting better, and at one point they had to open him up again and let him heal from the inside out. So for several days, Charlie walked around with an open wound under his sterile gauze dressing, and if you looked under the dressing and closely enough, you could see straight into his gut. I thought he would be thrilled by the repulsiveness

of this, by its resemblance to science fiction. He seemed embarrassed by it.

This particular week, we arrive on his usual day, but it's not
the taciturn Taiwanese surgeon who operated on him. Instead,
it's another transplant surgeon who is white, stocky, and balding
prematurely.

"*Hola!*" he says, before the exam room door is fully open,
before he even looks up from the chart he's reading. "Charlie
O'Doyle? You Charlie O'Doyle? Age twenty-nine?"

"That's me," Charlie says, half-naked and supine on the exam
table.

"How's it going?" The doctor's words come out of his mouth
in short, quick bursts. He is so clearly not from Iowa—*New York*,
I think, *definitely New York*—and he is so clearly a surgeon. Even
though he is short and only a little thick, his movements take up
so much space in the room. And not in that clumsy way, but in
the exacting, confident way of a man who is used to wielding a
scalpel. This guy was born to be a surgeon.

I'm observing him from a chair in the corner, and for the first
five minutes, I'm pretty sure he has no idea I'm here.

"You're the hero?" he asks Charlie.

"Pardon?" Charlie says.

"The hero. That's what I call the donors, because if you think
about it, that's what you are. You've saved a life. You know, heroes."

I can tell by Charlie's half-smile that he is more amused than
impressed by this guy's schtick. Charlie's eyes follow the doctor as
he moves back and forth across the room with caffeinated energy.
His blue scrubs swish between his legs when he walks.

The surgeon, who does not even introduce himself, looks

down at Charlie's open wound and says, "Hay-oh! What do we have here? Got infected, eh?"

"Yeah," Charlie says.

"Ouch," the doctor says, leaning in for a closer look. He sucks in air through his teeth. "How's the recipient look?"

"Well, you can ask her yourself. She's right there." Charlie nods to me, and the surgeon finally turns around to find me there.

"You?" he says. He looks me up and down, his eyes cutting down my body like a knife.

I nod.

He jumps back around to Charlie and doesn't even ask me who I am or how Charlie and I are connected. Nothing.

"How did you get roped into that?" the doctor says.

"I thought the drugs would be better," Charlie says, quite honestly. And it's true. He listened carefully about the morphine pump through the whole evaluation process, but when it came to pass, he was disappointed. The drugs just dulled his pain and put him to sleep. They didn't give him any of the hallucinations he was hoping for.

"Perks! Ha!" The surgeon snorts and looks like he's going to give Charlie a frat boy high-five or something. "Sweet." He presses on the flesh around Charlie's wound with his gloved hands, asking Charlie if it hurts. Every once in a while, Charlie's leg jerks up off the table like he's being electrocuted.

"Yow-za!" Charlie yells once.

"Let's seal this puppy up." I don't listen as he tends to Charlie and gives him the horrendous details of what he's about to do. "You might want to look away when I do this. It's not going to feel good," he says as he dabs a metallic liquid on the wound.

"Curses!" Charlie yells, like an old angry man, tightening his face, gripping the sides of the table with his fists. I don't know if I should run to him or stay where I am. I angle my head from behind the surgeon's body so I can see if Charlie needs me, but I can't get past the white lab coat. As he keeps electrocuting Charlie, he tries to talk, like the way dentists try to talk to you as they drill in your mouth.

"So, I always ask heroes this. I just want to know. Would you do it again?"

Now I listen. This guy is upfront. He's got the audacity to ask this in front of me the recipient, in front of Charlie's one true love. I want to clarify things for him. Charlie wasn't recruited for this. I didn't ask him for anything. No, this was an act of love.

Charlie lets out a weighty sigh and turns his face to the wall. "No. No, I don't think I would."

He keeps facing the pale pink wall while the doctor puts his hands all over him. Meanwhile, I'm frozen in the chair. I have a supportive smile across my face, but I feel it slowly sliding downward, though I try to keep it up. Charlie is trying to hold his grunts in now, pushing those sounds deep down in a place where they won't emerge. I lean over to see if I can see Charlie from the side of the doctor's coat. But an explanation doesn't follow. The paper on the table underneath Charlie crinkles every time he moves. The fluorescent lights are stark, buzzing.

The surgeon puts another dab of the painful solution on his skin, and when he does, I am the one who winces.

Chapter Eight

The ILLUSIVE SLEEP STEALER
and
HIS DANCING COCKATOOS

. . .

SLEEP IS SLOWLY BEING STOLEN FROM ME. I TRY TO HUNT DOWN the thief, but all I can come up with are the usual suspects: medications, the seasonal changes, the burrito for dinner. I blame it on these things, but when I lie in bed, I know what keeps me up. Charlie's frank admission has been on repeat in my head ever since we left the doctor's office that morning, like a song that you hate to hear but can't get out of your head. A week after that appointment, we still don't talk about what he said. Charlie and I walk around the tiny apartment, dodging each other in the hall; I squeeze my shoulders into my body as I pass.

During Charlie's long bout with post-surgery constipation and the pain from an infected incision, a large envelope came in the mail, and in it was a diploma-looking certificate that acknowledged Charles Kritvise O'Doyle for giving what they called "The Gift of Life." A grand, formal thing, it was printed on thick ivory parchment paper and embossed with the hospital seal. I told Charlie we should frame it and hang it in the living room.

"Please, Moonface," Charlie said, looking at me as if I had said something in poor taste.

"What do you want, Charlie? A medal?"

"Hardy-har," he said, listlessly.

I knew the piece of paper was indeed ridiculous, trivializing not just what Charlie did but also what the transplant meant for us. But the document was inaccurate. It was not just my life he had saved, but also our lives together. He was committing to our partnership. To me, this was more like a marriage certificate.

To hear Charlie say that he wouldn't do it again was like hearing him change his mind about the whole procedure, like him taking back what he had already entrusted with me. And though that wasn't possible, it felt like something—something heavier, more substantial than a mere kidney—was being ripped from me.

ONCE, WHILE SITTING AT DIALYSIS IN A CENTER, I REMEMBER AN old woman in the treatment chair next to me talking about another patient who used to come to dialysis regularly before she got a kidney from her daughter.

"I would never do that," my neighbor said, running a hand through her thick afro. "Ask my daughter for a kidney."

"Why not?" asked a nurse, who was hooking her up to the machine.

"I'd be too worried that she would need that kidney later. And it's just not fair to put someone through a surgery like that. What a waste it would be if it didn't work! I wouldn't be able to take it."

At the time, I heard her words, but I couldn't look past what Charlie was willing to do for us. I couldn't look past what his offer meant to our relationship. But if I believed that something magical had happened that morning in August—not transplant but transcendence—then I had to believe that something could be undone when or if something went wrong, if I did reject him. That this was our bodies telling us that maybe we weren't meant for each other, or that this wasn't meant to be.

Charlie's words play in my head, and in the early morning hours, I still can't get to bed. Lying here, I silently vow to keep this kidney, whatever it takes, to show Charlie what it means to me, that "The Gift of Life" was not given in vain.

AND JUST THEN . . .

MY BODY BEGINS TO SHIVER. IT'S A CRISP NIGHT IN OCTOBER, and I'm woken up from a vague dream in which I'm riding a rickety roller coaster and feeling the old wooden track tossing me around in the small metal car. I wake up to realize that my body is shaking outside this dream, too. Tensing up my arms and legs, I try to make the tremors stop. I pull up the wooly blankets from the foot of the bed and try to lie still.

"What's wrong with you, Moonface?" Charlie asks, squinting through the darkness to look at me.

"I'm co-o-o-ld."

"You're always so cold. You don't wear enough layers." In the haze of the dimly lit room, he gets up, his hair pointing in all directions, and brings me my pink bathrobe from the bathroom. I sit up in bed, and he pulls the robe over my arms and around my back, and almost all in a one-shot camera move, he glides over to the closet in the other room and pulls out our old, green, zero-degree sleeping bag, the one we camped out on in Big Sur and snuggled up in along the rim of the Grand Canyon. He puts the bag over me and pushes its edges under my legs and under my arms.

The shivering is not normal, but I don't tell him this. If something is wrong with the kidney, I want to take care of it first, before he can possibly know. I will call the doctor's office in the morning.

"You're that cold?" he asks, in disbelief.

"It's just the change in seasons, I guess." I try to keep my teeth from chattering.

"Here," he says, more annoyed than suspicious, and he holds the layers over me, so tight, until I can't shake anymore, until he is practically lying on top of me with all his weight, pushing down my body and suppressing all that's going wrong with it. He eventually falls asleep like this, and I lift one shoulder until he slides off the slick sleeping bag and back to his side of the bed.

I get some sleep in little sparks between my worry and the actual trembling, but in the morning I cannot control the chills at all despite how much I focus on a sight in the room—the lamp, the window blind. I get up and retch in the bathroom, over the toilet. I crawl through the apartment, clinging to the walls with my hands.

Charlie already left for work, leaving while I was still asleep. My heart is beating in my head, which is never a good sign. I look in the mirror, and there is sweat on my forehead and on my nose. I pull the thermometer from a cup in the bathroom and put it in my mouth. But before it goes in, I already know what the temperature will be. I sit on the couch and call the transplant clinic.

"Well, sweetie. You taking care of our patient? How's he doin'?" LuAnn, our nurse, answers. She loves Charlie. He charmed her the first day they met by looking at her beehive of a head and telling her she looked just like Tammy Wynette, but so much more independent! She blushed.

"He's fine. He started work today." I hear my voice quivering.

"Oh, good. He's not lifting anything, is he? We don't need him lifting anything. He doesn't have to be a He-Man. But I think he knows that," she laughs to herself. She speaks so brightly that for a minute, I think that this drain I'm falling into is a dream, that the reality is that things are as delightful as her voice sounds. But I tell her about the uncontrollable shaking and the sweats this morning.

"Back pain?" she asks, and though I think it is unrelated, last week, I remember asking Charlie to rub my back, which was sore from what I thought was hunching over my desk too long. I had asked him to go to the store and buy me heating pads.

"Uh, huh." LuAnn thinks for a while. "Temp?"

"A hundred and one point eight," I read from the digital thermometer.

She pauses. Her silence gives me more reason to worry.

"Yes, you should probably come into the clinic today, just so the doctors can take a look at you. Just come on down as soon as you can. You don't need an appointment. I'll be here."

I tell myself to hold it together, that the fever could be nothing. Something they could treat with an aspirin. *Just get to the clinic. Just don't worry yet, just get to the clinic.* I'm in the bathroom pulling my hair up in a ponytail when the phone rings again. I pick it up in the bedroom, and on the line LuAnn says, "Okay, sweetie, you know what? Come to think of it, I know what the doctor's going to say. I might as well get you ready for it. With a temp like that, they're probably going to admit you. So you might as well bring a bag of clothes and come straight to Admissions."

• • •

IT'S NOT LUANN WHO MEETS ME IN THE LOBBY OF THE HOSPITAL, but a nurse who whisks me upstairs back to the transplant ward where I have been before and tells me to get out of my clothes and into the standard hospital gear. She swings the door of a room wide open and shuffles me inside. There is one bed.

"A single?" I turn to her.

"Yes," she says, a smile escaping her lips, because she knows a single is what you want in the hospital when you're not feeling your best. Another person with just a paper-thin curtain next to you is probably the least of your worries, but it's appreciated when you are crying, half-naked, out of frustration. I get myself up on the bed and put my head down on the pillow, and as I lie down, I see that the nurse puts an ISOLATION sign on the front of the open door.

"I'm contagious?" I ask her.

"Maybe. I don't have any reports yet," she says, before shutting the door and making me feel like she's locking me in a cage.

Contagious? Shivering? What can it be now? *They are just being cautious*, I think, with the ISOLATION sign, worrying more about what can come into the room than what is going out. The anti-rejection drugs that suppress my immune system make me susceptible to more than the average folk, especially in a hospital. So maybe that sign is there to protect me, not to protect others from me. I don't know. I pull off my clothes quickly and try to settle into bed so as to distract myself from the myriad possibilities.

The room is small with a slim window in front of the bed. An off-white phone with a long cord hangs from a movable table. I hesitate calling Charlie. I don't want to tell him that I am back in the hospital for I don't know what or that his kidney could possibly be in trouble. A three-month-old transplant, already gone kaput.

Charlie's been working with special-ed students at the local high school, and when I call for him, the school secretary pulls him out of class so he can use the phone in the main office.

"Is this my mail-order bride?" he says when he picks up.

I don't tell him much, just that I have a fever and that the chills from the last few nights were probably something more that my just being cold.

"I knew it!" he says, practically spitting into the phone. "Damn it. I'll be right there."

Chapter Nine

The CELEBRATED and ADORED ROYAL FILIPINO MIND READER

· · ·

I N WALKS THIS ATTRACTIVE BLONDE WEARING A SHINY NAVY AND red sweatsuit. She's not sweating, though, and I think she has wandered into the wrong room when she takes a seat on my bed and looks me square in the eyes. I'm ready to press the call button and tell the nurse that a nutcase has gotten past security and is now threatening my safety. She sounds authentic, but doctors are never this pretty or this stylish, and they certainly never have time to work out. I take my hand off the call button, and when I reach out to shake her hand, it is surprisingly warm.

"Pardon the outfit," she says. "I just got a page about you when I was coming back from an aerobics class." She doesn't smell like sweat. She smells like raspberries. I'll state right now that she was the best-smelling doctor I've ever met. Warm hands, fruit-scented. Again suspicious.

She introduces herself as an infectious-disease doctor, and I say, "I'm infected?"

"We're just covering our bases," she says, not committing to any diagnoses at first. She briefly reviews my medical history. "But what's been going on lately?"

"Well, a couple weeks ago, I had a pretty bad headache. I thought it was my sinuses. This weekend, I had a terrible back pain." I lean forward and point to the back of my hips where my native kidneys still are. I tell her about the fever this morning and the cold sweats of the last few weeks. I tell her everything. I want to know if I get to keep Charlie's kidney. So I don't leave anything out. I tell her about how I've been forgetting things, how I can't keep my head straight. I don't leave out the night sweats. Or the shivers. Or my fears. "I can't lose this kidney."

"We don't know that yet," she says. In my highest hopes, I don't think you call in an infectious-disease doctor if it's a problem with your transplanted kidney. Right? "We'll figure out what's going on," she says, with the raspberry smell trailing behind her as she leaves the room.

IF IT'S NOT PARENTAL INSTINCT, THEN IT'S MY MOTHER'S FILIPINO superpowers, or maybe God speaking through the GPS system in my father's car. Whatever it is, my parents have found a way to detect when I am sick and how they can find me. It's their own little honing device. Sometimes it takes only an unanswered phone call, or a crack in my voice, or a cough, but the minute they sense something is wrong, they get in their SUV and they start driving toward me, wherever I am.

Once, in college, my father called my roommate on a random Tuesday night and she told him an ambulance had just left and taken me to the emergency room with stomach cramps. I was planning on calling them when I knew what was happening, if it was indeed something serious, but there my father went, my mother in the car with him, in his Acura down Interstate 70, ninety miles an hour from Pittsburgh to Baltimore.

"My baby!" my mother must've yelled from the passenger seat, as they raced at breakneck speeds toward me.

When a cop pulled my father over somewhere in Hancock, Maryland, my father looked squarely at the cop and gave it to him straight: "My baby's in the emergency room. You can call the hospital yourself if you'd like." My father is neither an annoying nor intimidating man, but when he is serious about something, he will most likely get it. He handed the cop his big chunky cell phone with his finger ready to dial the number, but the officer, seeing that there was no stopping this man from getting to Baltimore as quickly as he could, said, "It's okay, sir, but you'll have to drive more carefully than that. I'm sure she wants to see you, but she'll probably prefer to see you alive."

"Yes. Thank you, officer," was all my gracious father said, before pushing his foot back down on the pedal.

IT IS NO SURPRISE WHEN MY PARENTS WALK INTO MY HOSPITAL room one night out of breath. I can smell my mother's perfume from down the hall. When they walk into the room, my mother is the one who seems exhausted, even though I know it was my father who was driving, pulling through the night traffic all by himself while she slept in the passenger seat.

I complain when they arrive because I don't want to feel like I need them. When I see them storming through the door, I feel once again like that scared eighteen-year-old who is uncertain about what's happening to her.

"Could you please leave?" I ask them.

"You shouldn't talk to us like that," my mother says.

The phone rings and my mother answers; it's my brother calling from New York. I'm too tired to lift the receiver or to talk. I push away everything she puts near my pillow—her rosary, the phone—all in dramatic fashion.

"She's got a high fever. She's delirious!" my mother vents to my brother. I roll my eyes and hold my tongue. "No, I don't think she's crazy . . . but we're just trying to find out what's wrong with her."

I AM STILL SHIVERING. MY FEVER HAS YET TO BE CONTROLLED, and it still makes me tremble, making the bed rock, all its little parts—the rails, the up-and-down mechanisms, the frame underneath. They all shake. I press the call button for the nurse, and when over the small speaker they ask me what I need, I tell them that I'm shivering. It sounds like this:

"I'm sh-sh-sh-hivering. My fever."

"We'll call the doctor to see what you can do," the nurse says. "How do you feel?"

"Like I'm in a scene from *The Exorcist*," I say. "I'm trying to keep my head from spinning off."

But when she puts the needle into the IV, I can feel my body suddenly relax and I can feel all my muscles slowly ease. My body loosens and the shaking miraculously stops.

DAYS PASS. SEVEN, TO BE EXACT. LONGER THAN WHEN I WAS IN the hospital with the surgery. The tests are unending, as is the parade of student doctors who duck in at all hours of the day and ask me questions I have definitely answered before.

There are days that feel normal. There has been a revolving door of guests all wearing the smocks that are provided for the isolation room. My mother and father cover the days when Charlie is busy at work, then Charlie comes in the evenings after work and, sometimes, stays long after visiting hours are over. The nurses, who find him charming and sweet, pretend not to see him once the intercom asks all the guests to leave.

"I don't want you to ever feel alone," he says, in all seriousness. And he sits on the vinyl chair beside me and we watch an old rerun of M*A*S*H on the TV hanging from the wall. He stays as long as he can before he starts nodding off to sleep and I have to send him home.

Someone is usually with me, but sometimes there are gaps, like when my parents have to go to church, as they have been going daily, and when Charlie is still at work. He's made new friends at his new job, and I tell him to go out with them once in a while to get to know them.

"I don't want them to think that you spend all your free time in a hospital caring for your sick girlfriend," I tell him.

"But I do," he says.

"If only you knew what you were getting into," I say.

"If only . . ." he says with false regret. Or regret.

DURING ONE OF THOSE GAP MOMENTS, A RADIOLOGY TECHNIcian comes up to my room to take yet another chest x-ray. I don't ask what for anymore. I just assume they like sending radiation through my body, that there's a collection of my entire skeletal structure in a file somewhere and they need just one more photo to complete it. There have been so many tests in the past few days that I just assume they are still collecting data. I just want them to tell me that it is definitely not my kidney, and they don't do that. They don't say anything about that.

The tech has a thick mustache and a brown mullet, and he rolls in a giant machine. His muscles bulge through his lab coat.

"Ugh," I grunt.

"I know, sorry," he says, in a high voice that is incongruent with his build.

I am too weak these days to make it down to the radiology department myself. They've been coming to me. Charlie says I should feel special by the room service, but I don't. The tech uses his big muscles to lift me to the side of the bed so my scrawny, dry legs hang off the edge of the railing. He lines up the bulky side of the machine against my chest and asks me to breathe in and hold it. When I do, my lungs fill with air and my bladder suddenly feels heavy.

"Just one more time," he yells from behind the curtain. And when I inhale again, my bladder feels heavier. I think I can make it to the bathroom, but I'll have to drag the long IV pole that's attached to my arm. I'll have to unplug the IV machine from the wall, sling it around the other side of the bed, and take a few steps to the bathroom. In my head, I'm mapping out the steps and the time it will take me to accomplish them. *Come on, man.*

"Okay, that's all we need," he says.

"Good." I say that I've got to use the restroom. The bladder presses down heavier.

"Uh, hold on there, dear." He pushes his x-ray machine, but its cord gets caught under my bed. The IV pole is trapped back in the corner. I'm up, and I try to tug the pole loose.

"Wait," the tech says, as he dislodges his machine. But I can't. My bladder feels huge and I try to see if I can reach over to the bathroom with my IV arm sticking out of the door because I'm gonna go soon. But it won't reach. I put my hand between my legs, thinking that will stop the pee, but it doesn't, and I feel the warm stream filling my pajama pants and hissing its way onto the floor.

The tears stream down almost as quickly. "I didn't make it," I say, in barely a whisper. The man is uncomfortable and shocked. He's pushing his x-ray machine out the door, and he tries to look away but suddenly gets nervous, and says, "I'll tell your nurse." I know he just wants to get the hell out of that room, and away from me, and I don't blame him.

I am helpless. This is what I have become now—a soggy mess on the floor, a woman who can't control her body.

MY FATHER DROPS OFF MY MOTHER AND LEAVES TO GRAB SOME dinner. I can hear her voice from far away, and when she rounds the corner into my room, she is smiling. But the corners of her mouth drop when she sees me crying.

"What, what is it?" she says.

"Oh, it's just too much. I need Charlie."

"Where is Charlie?"

"I don't know. At work?" The room still smells like piss, which makes it worse.

"So, what's wrong?" she asks, throwing her purse on the chair.

"Oh, I don't know." I collapse into bed in new pajamas, my head in her arms like a child. I lie there like this even after an orderly has mopped the floor, even after my father has come up from the parking lot with armfuls of take-out boxes and my mother has shooed him away. I imagine he is in a waiting room somewhere, giving us space.

When I finally come up for air, she says, "What, *anak*?"

"The kidney," I tell her.

"You're not losing Charlie's kidney," she reassures me.

"We don't know that."

"Well, is it that? Is that what you're afraid of?" she asks.

"Yes," I say, "maybe this was a mistake. Maybe this transplant shouldn't have happened."

My mother takes a box of tissues from a drawer in the bedside table.

"If I lose this kidney . . ." I start.

"What's going to happen to you and Charlie?" she finishes.

The roots of my mother's black hair are turning gray. You can't really tell from afar, but I am so close to her now, I can see them. She hasn't been home for weeks, so she hasn't had them done. And now her eyes are thick with tears. I am making her look old.

"Ay!" she sighs. "I knew this would happen."

"Mom!" I don't want to hear an I-told-you-so moment from her right now.

"No," she says, continuing to rub my head. "I knew it would be hard." She seems annoyed by the situation now, making *tsk* sounds under her breath. "You think you have to feel everything he feels, huh?

"Look," she says, taking off her glasses and folding them into her hands. "You were twenty-eight when you and Charlie were transplanted, right? When you committed to help one another." She pauses. "When I was twenty-eight, I married your father in a church in Manila."

This I know. I'm afraid that she's going to tell me the story of their meeting. It's strange when you find out your parents have a Romeo and Juliet past. A skinny kid from Manila with a nice smile, my father was always sweet. When he laughed, no sounds came out, just a warm subtle grin. My mother was so different then, coming from a wealthy family in Manila, the daughter of a prominent lawyer, who was in the inner circles of President Ferdinand Marcos. President Aquino, too. Filipino royalty. My mother was the second of four sisters, and as she describes, "I was the funny one." I can almost imagine her and her insult comedy. She tells me over and over again the story of how she and my father met. They were in the same class in medical school before my mother dropped out. It's a good story, but it's not exactly what I want to hear now.

Nor do I want to hear about how my father made it to the States. He came to New York City in 1969 and worked in a blood bank on Bleecker Street. When he finally saved up enough money to get an apartment in Massachusetts and airfare from the Philippines, he flew my mother over. In our old photo albums, there are black-and-white pictures of her deplaning a TWA bird, with her bouffant of a hairdo and a very American-looking suit. She was going to be a doctor's wife. In America.

"I know, Mom!" I say. I don't need an encore.

"I know you know. But what you didn't know was this. When I came here I was so alone. I didn't know anybody. I wanted to go home. I cried in the apartment all day while your dad was at work. It was hard, *anak*. But I had to come here because your father was here, and he was doing what he always wanted to do. He was sad for me, but he had to keep working. And he needed me to be here with him.

"Sometimes love is sacrifice, babe. And sometimes, you just have to live with that, whether you are the one sacrificing or not."

I pull the bed sheet up to my face to try to keep my nose from running. There's a lot I want to say, but not to my mother. Not right now. I think: *He gave me his kidney. I owe it to him to keep it. I don't want him to regret this. What is this between me and Charlie now? What have I done? I am ruining a solid relationship.*

"Of course, this is still a love story," my mother continues, like she is reading my mind. "Can you imagine? Giving your body to someone else purely because you love that person? I think you forget sometimes that these people—your brother, Charlie—they are trying to save you. They have sacrificed for you. I think you forget how sick you really were. This miraculous transplant saved you from getting worse. From maybe dying, *anak*. Yes, it means Charlie loves you because he gave you a kidney, but if it doesn't take, that doesn't mean anything about his love. You might feel bad because he feels bad. But he gave you this so you can go back to being you. Now think. This is your body. Your mind. Who is this person I made?

"Of course, this is love. But this is also your story. This is about how you survived. How you are surviving. Charlie is doing fine. Now is not the time to worry about him. How are you going to get through this? *You*," she says, pointing to me.

Chapter Ten

An AMERICAN RAGTIME ORCHESTRA PLAYS the TUNES of LOVE

. . .

B Y DAY TWELVE OF THE UNKNOWN DISEASE, EVERYONE LOOKS exhausted. My mother has worn her thumbprint into the wooden rosary beads that she hides deep inside her shirtsleeve. My father's already droopy eyes sag even farther down his face. These days, my parents and Charlie look like wilted flowers propped up against the walls of my hospital room. They come to life only when a doctor comes in, but shrivel back down when still no diagnosis just means more tests.

So much for magic, so much for our cells combining and our souls converging. I look at Charlie longingly at times, hoping that the kidney stays, that Charlie feels better, and that the love between us is real. My mother doesn't know what Charlie said at the doctor's office, and I don't want to tell her. But when I replay his words in my head, I can almost feel my body dissolving, the very tissue that holds us together coming apart.

. . .

WHEN BLONDIE FINALLY EXPLAINS WHAT I HAVE, HER DIAGNOSIS doesn't make sense to me.

"*Histoplasmosis,*" she says again, this time slower.

"Fungal?" my father the physician says, looking surprised.

"It's a fungal infection that we often see here in the Ohio Valley. The spores are in the air and usually come from bat or bird droppings. Now, have you been eating animal droppings?" Blondie jokes.

"Bat shit?" I say. "No."

"Whoa!" Charlie perks up. While the thought of bat shit invading my system is grossing out everyone in the room, I am sure that Charlie is mesmerized by the possibility of this. He's probably wondering if people take bat shit as a hallucinogen.

"I'm just kidding. Usually we see it in farmers because they spend so much time in the dirt," Blondie says.

My mother jumps out of her seat: "They live in the basement!" She points at me and Charlie as she talks. "They breathe in dirt all the time. I knew it. See? I told you."

Blondie laughs and says, "We all get it. It's in the air. But most of us have the immune system to fight it off." She turns to face me again. "But you don't."

"Lucky me."

"Lucky you. With all those immunosuppressants we're giving you for the transplant, the fungus found a nice place to stay. Your immunity is suppressed because of all the anti-rejection drugs, so you probably got what everyone gets, but we are just better at fighting the disease off."

"So, I can go home now?"

"Not quite," she says. "We're going to have to give you some heavy-duty antibiotics for a heavy-duty infection like this. We'll give them to you through an IV."

"I know what *that* means."

"You'll be in here for a while longer until we can get these drugs working. It will take a while for your body to respond. You might still have the fevers. But you'll still be here so we can watch them."

OUTSIDE, THE AIR ALREADY LOOKS A LITTLE BIT CRISPER. WHEN Charlie comes to visit, the skin underneath his stubble is rosy and his curly blond hair looks windblown. Now that we know what is wrong with me, we know how to treat it. My parents are still in Iowa with us, but roaming around the town less frantically than they were before. My father can't stop talking about the hotel where they are staying.

Later that night, the smell of chicken patties and mashed potatoes lingers in the hall. I'm repulsed by the odor, but live with it for now because I feel like this situation is temporary. I'm going home soon. They'll give me medicine through an IV for a few weeks and then they'll eventually send me home.

My parents have left for the night, getting ready to head back to Pittsburgh in a few days. My father has fewer things to worry about, so he stops fussing over me and instead starts calling his office at home and worrying about his patients there. Sometimes, when he does feel moved to talk, he doesn't discuss my health with me. Instead, he sticks to talking about the hotel in which he has stayed for several weeks. He says that this little dinky hotel in Iowa has been his most favorite hotel in his whole life. His whole life! He swears. "The hardboiled eggs are boiled just right," he says.

• • •

BLONDIE WARNS ME THAT EVEN THOUGH THE DOCTORS HAVE identified the disease and are beginning to treat it, the effects of the medication won't be seen for a few days.

"You still might be getting the same symptoms for a while," she says. "So, we'll keep you here just a little longer. We'll keep the nurses checking on you."

As Charlie and I sit in silence, I feel my legs start to shake, and then my shoulders. It's one of those fevers again when the shaking will not stop. I need a shot of Demerol to make it stop. I try to tell Charlie this, but all that comes out is "Ch-Ch-Char—"

He notices only when the rail of the bed starts shaking. He turns. "The fever! Hold on," he says, pressing down on my arms to hold them still.

He presses the nurses' call button. "Nurse! She needs the shot!" he says into the box.

"We'll be right there," a grainy voice answers.

I can't stop shaking. Even my head writhes on the pillow, and Charlie puts a hand on my forehead to keep it still. I know these are the lasting effects of the virus. I know this is the end of it. If I didn't keep these ideas in my head, I would be panicking now.

Charlie holds me down but screams out the door this time into the hall.

"*Hello?!*"

The male nurse comes in, concerned, but holding nothing.

"She needs the shot! *Give her* the shot!" Charlie screams, in a role reminiscent of Shirley MacLaine.

"Right," the nurse says. He turns and returns with just what I need. And Charlie stays there with me until the shaking stops, until I'm fast asleep.

• • •

THE NEXT NIGHT, THE ROOM IS EMPTY AND I TURN OFF THE LIGHT over the bed so only the last fading rays of the sun come through the windows. I don't hear any alarms or call buttons down the hall. It's almost peaceful. I think that this is the quietest place I've been in a while.

I breathe and exhale purposefully. Again. I have never liked the idea of being alone in a hospital room. When I was young, I would almost panic if I found myself in a space like this, in this vulnerable cave that invites in people who want to deconstruct your parts, to break you down. I always thought that it was better to have someone there who knew how to put you back together again. The right way.

"Meditating?"

I open my eyes to Charlie's familiar face, his reddish stubble now grown into a full beard, his eyes catching the reflection of sun. He is dreamy.

The male nurse pops in after Charlie nestles into a chair. "Need anything?" he says.

"No, I've got everything I need," I tell him.

"So, everything is going to be fine," Charlie says.

"I'm so happy I'm not losing this kidney."

"Yeah, 'cause I don't have another one to give."

"Not that you would give it up." It just comes out, like a piercing knife that you accidentally toss in the direction of a friend.

"Excuse me?" Charlie says, daring me to repeat it. "Is that what you think?"

I look down at the ground.

"Why would you say that, Moon?"

"You told that doctor that you regret it."

"No, I said I wouldn't do it again," he clarifies.

"Same thing."

"No, it's not," he says louder now, his voice in a deadlock with mine.

"Then why did you say it?"

He pauses. His sneakers squeak against the newly mopped floor as he steps closer and then farther, like he's trying to find a good place to stop.

"Man, Moonface, everything about that surgery hurt like a bitch. If I had to go through it again, it might drive me crazy." Even as he says it now, grimacing as he remembers, I start to sink in the bed, my body feeling like deadweight.

"You know, Charlie, I've been wondering what it would be like if I never got this kidney, if I just stayed on dialysis. I mean, maybe I was being greedy or selfish. Maybe I could have stayed on dialysis forever, and we wouldn't have to worry about this."

"Well, you hated dialysis, and no one is worrying about this but you."

I can hear the anger in his voice rising, and it worries me more now that I'm worrying too much. He stands up and turns around like he's going to leave, and then turns back toward me. "Why are you so insane? Why do you and that crazy surgeon worry about what you would do different? What if it never happened? What if you just stayed on dialysis forever? What if we never met? What if I never got drunk and hit on you that night? What's the use in wondering? We'll never know."

"I just think it would be easier sometimes."

"So after all this, after all that we've been through, after we know everything is going to be okay, now you're going to take a second look at this? We didn't do this transplant so we could look back all the time. We've got to look forward, Moonface. You want to get out of here? You want to quit worrying about your health?"

"I don't want to be sick anymore," I tell him.

"Okay," he says, sounding somewhat relieved.

"I just want a normal life," I continue.

"Okay. What else do you want? I'll get it for you."

"I want us to be crazy in love," I say.

"Well, you're crazy. And I'm in love," he says, easing into a dreamy smile.

"And while I'm at it, I want to get married. I want babies. I want little Charlie O'Doyles walking around in sailor suits."

"Well," he leans in close so we're almost touching noses, "you ain't gonna get that. Not with me. I have big plans for us. Next summer we're hopping freight trains across Canada. This winter, we're buying a motorcycle with a side car and we're touring all over the French Alps." Then he stands back and waits for me to fill in the next line.

ACT III

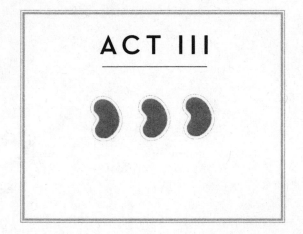

Chapter Eleven

The FAMOUS MINSTRELS of BALTIMORE UNDER EXCLUSIVE ENGAGEMENT in MOONFACE'S HEAD

. . .

AFTER I GRADUATE, I ASK CHARLIE WHAT'S NEXT FOR US. "TELL me where you want to go, Charlie. Seriously, I'll take you anywhere." I am cocky now, with a masters degree under my belt and a body that works. "Freight trains? For real?"

"I'm tired, Moonface," Charlie says. "Let's go home." He slouches into the couch and from the look on his face, I know he means "home" as in "easy," where we can take a breath. I know he means Baltimore. While it hasn't technically been our home for a long time, it is a welcoming place to return, it's close to our families and friends, and it's familiar.

Just like when we moved to Iowa, we pull into our new city with all our belongings in yet another neatly packed rented truck—how easily our possessions and organs move from one place to the next. As we head east toward where the states huddle in a corner of the map, I already miss Iowa's wide open spaces, its white lawn chairs in high grass, its lacy curtain hems sweeping against the windowsills. But here the lush green lawns of the Midwest are replaced by the gray concrete of Baltimore. The idleness of broad Iowa streets is replaced by the swift and jerky movements of trains, cars, and even bikers who pop themselves high over their seats and lunge into traffic without fear.

It's as if those bikers embrace the message on the posters that hang from every building in the city—BELIEVE, the signs read in thick white letters against a plain black background. They hang from some of the city's largest office buildings, from the windows of the skinny brick houses, from hotel canopies, and from City Hall. Smaller versions are on the bumpers of minivans and sporty wagons.

"Wow! This city really encourages its football team," I tell Charlie when we pass yet another BELIEVE, thinking that the colors clearly resemble those of the city's local NFL team.

"I don't think those have anything to do with football," Charlie snorts. Later, we find out that the signs are actually the mayor's campaign to fight drugs. How better to fight the city's increasing drug problem than to make its citizens *believe* it can happen? What else to do but post signs everywhere reminding citizens that believing is enough? The audacity of this little city, to think it can fight one of the nation's largest epidemics. I kind of like its ambition.

Unlike that apartment we had in Iowa, which was low and flat, our apartment here is high and narrow. It has only a few rooms, and I'm sure in our apartment hunting there were larger, more spacious options within our price range, but I liked the old glamour of it: the red-painted walls, the marble non-working fireplace, and the ever-entertaining pocket doors. In our new apartment, I wake up in the mornings and stretch my arms by the window to see a BELIEVE sign hanging from the school across the street, and I begin to like the city more and more.

Charlie is not only sick of gallivanting around the country; he is sick of having crappy jobs. We sit on the terrace of a coffee shop, and Charlie plays with his cocktail napkin, folding and refolding it into different shapes. "I need to start something," he says.

"Maybe you should start writing again," I say, knowing that he already has. I've seen the notebooks of handwritten pages piling up by his bedside. "Go back to school."

"Yeah," he says, still fidgeting with the tabletop origami.

"What do you want to do?"

"Write," he says, "draw, read, sing, make dioramas . . ."

"Then you should," I say.

I know how he feels. Now that I have the time, I'm ready to focus my energy toward a project. I take a part-time adjunct teaching position at a community college to make ends meet, and on the days I don't teach, I pull out a folder of old essay drafts I wrote in school. I sit at my desk at the window and leaf through them, trying to feel a spark.

Beth calls almost every week and gives me updates on what is happening with the people we know: who's getting published, who's moving where, who's dating whom. She also tells me that a woman who graduated before us is expecting.

"Whoa!" I shout into the receiver. "A baby?"

"Yup!" Beth says.

I rub my belly and imagine something growing there. I'm wearing skin-tight jeans and a tank top, so this image exercises all my imagination. I arch my back and push my belly out, and it doesn't feel as uncomfortable as I thought it would.

Beth tries to think of more gossip. "Let's see," she sings.

I realize that if I want to know anything about what's going on with her life, I'm going to have to ask her point blank.

"How are you and the professor doing?"

She pauses on the phone, and then confesses: "We might buy a house together."

"What?!" I shriek.

"Do you think we should?" she asks, sounding like she just needs one nudge more to commit.

"Yes! So, what does this mean? Are you just playing along?"

"No," she says firmly, "I think we should buy a house together. I think I like having him around."

Apparently they tried to work out some scheme where he would sell his little house and move in with her, or where she would sell her little house and move in with him. But after talking to a real estate agent, it made more sense to sell both of the little houses and buy a bigger house that they would both fit into comfortably.

"What if you guys got married?" I tease her.

"What if *you* guys got married?" she snaps back.

"What if you guys got pregnant?" I say.

"What if *you* guys got pregnant?" she says.

Then the two of us hang on the line silently, one waiting for the other to say something.

In the fall, Charlie starts a graduate program in writing and publishing arts at a university nearby. It seems perfect for him: he shapes his drafts into stories, then turns around and creates what he calls a "physical container" for them.

"One might call such a container a book?" I suggest, as I watch him sitting on the floor, cutting figures out of magazine pages and pasting them into a shoebox.

"Yeah, one might say that. But a book isn't always pages collected and bound. Sometimes, it's a video you watch. Sometimes it's a box with pictures. Sometimes it's something you haven't even thought of yet." He turns away from me and dives into another magazine with a pair of scissors.

Charlie is often gone in the first few months after we get to Baltimore, sometimes in the computer lab at school or in class or at a bar talking shop with his classmates. I get home from teaching some afternoons and have the place to myself. I make myself a pot of coffee, open up my folder of drafts, and force myself to pick one, just one, page to rework. But I don't. The damn window keeps catching my eye, or rather my skinny reflection in it. At first, when Beth told me about the pregnant woman in Iowa, I couldn't help but imagine how her life was changing: from being half of a couple to part of a family, from identifying herself as a writer to a mother, or both. Now when I think about her, I feel just a tinge of jealousy. And I find myself thinking about an unborn baby that doesn't even belong to me.

DURING OUR WINTER BREAK, WE FLY TO LAS VEGAS TO MEET UP with Beth and the professor and to stay with my former classmates Violet and Raj. Violet and Raj married in Iowa the summer after we came, then moved to the desert so Raj could start a writing fellowship. Raj, with his dark beard and his fashionable gray glasses, picks us up from the airport and grabs us like we're long-lost relatives. "Vegas sucks," he says. "I've been craving some intelligent forms of life."

When we get to their house, Beth, Violet, and the professor are already in their pajamas, laughing and smiling on the living room floor. We catch up on each other's lives, which, though miles from each other, seem somewhat parallel. Beth and the professor settled on their house—a mammoth, rehabbed Victorian on Washington Avenue. We tell them that we have started to look at buying a house somewhere in Baltimore, but nothing as giant as theirs. Raj is back in school getting his Ph.D., and Charlie is back in school working on his masters. They sit in the corner and talk about what's on each other's reading lists.

Violet says she wants to get pregnant.

"Me, too!" I spit out. It comes out of nowhere.

"Really?" she says. "We should get pregnant at the same time."

"Yes!" I say, arching my back again and pretending I'm already in my third trimester. "I would love to have a baby." This is the first time I say it out loud, and I feel that when I say it, I can't stuff it back in.

"Would you get married first?" Beth asks.

"I don't know yet," I say.

"Because I think we're getting married," she says, ". . . tomorrow."

I freeze. I look over at Violet, and she's nodding as if to confirm that Beth isn't joking.

"What?" Charlie yells from the corner.

The sneaky rascals have planned it out. We thought we were just spending New Year's Eve getting drunk on the Strip. But now we learn that we have a wedding to attend at a little white chapel presided over by an Elvis impersonator.

The next afternoon, I have to borrow a dress from Violet's expansive closet and buy shoes at the local department store. We buy bottles of champagne from the market and red roses for Beth to hold as she walks down the aisle. Before we head out for the chapel, Violet and I help Beth get dressed. She wears a clingy satin dress that comes up high on her legs, nothing like the shapeless tunics she usually wears. She looks slim and sexy, and Violet and I catcall her from the corner of the bathroom.

As we stand in the vestibule of the chapel, I whisper to her, "There's nothing ambivalent about that dress at all."

She turns around and winks at me before heading down the blue velvet aisle.

A MYSTERIOUS CRYING BEGINS NEXT DOOR TO OUR APARTMENT. I hear it in the afternoons when I am sitting on the couch. The wailing pierces through the brick wall in short bursts. I suspect a cat is trapped or a teakettle whistle has gone wonky, but before I have a chance to put a finger on the sound, it ends. I think that it might be my imagination, but once, Charlie hears it, too. He stops pasting together the pages of the book he is constructing and presses his ear against the wall behind the bed.

We don't yet know our neighbors, but sometimes when we hear their shoes stomping up the stairs, Charlie runs to the peephole on the front door and looks out. "Old lady with bad wig from the fourth floor," he whispers to me in the kitchen. "Biker dude in spandex." He has never once mentioned a pregnant woman or a baby.

Around the neighborhood, there are even more new sounds and sights emerging every day. At night, helicopter blades often sputter overhead like the city is being sprayed with bullets from an automatic weapon. The searchlights glare into our window while we sleep. Despite the chaos of Baltimore, it means something to me now: a whole new world, one free of surgeries or hospitals, trips to the emergency room. In another place, far from Iowa, it feels like there are things that can happen that I haven't even considered yet.

•   •   •

For instance: being inspired by an Elvis impersonator.

It is a moment that starts about as unromantically as you can get. Charlie and I are paying bills on the living room floor, sitting close to each other in the space between the coffee table and the couch. The rent for our spacious two-bedroom basement apartment in Iowa was almost half the rent of our one-bedroom with a narrow galley kitchen. Things are becoming tight. Money, too. Charlie has a full-time position at a nearby music conservatory, while still taking a full load of classes. As our bills begin to pile up, my health insurance from Iowa slowly begins to wind down. I've started looking for other plans, but insurance companies aren't particularly welcoming when you have kidney disease and when you've had two kidney transplants. Bills and envelopes are spread out on the hardwood between us like a heap of kindling, and Charlie suggests that we should get married.

"Right," I say, resting an elbow on the seat of the couch behind me. "Then I could kill you for the life insurance."

"I mean, we might as well," Charlie says, shrugging his shoulders. "And it was actually kind of sweet in Vegas. The tiny chapel, none of the fuss." I have not looked at Charlie closely in a while, the way his beard contours the sides of his face. His cheekbones are more defined now; he looks older. He is a man now, different from that young college boy with whom I escaped to Hawaii so many years ago.

I have never actually imagined the moment Charlie might propose or the wedding we might have. For years Charlie and I cleverly evaded the subject of marriage when our families brought it up, mostly because it meant that we had to start taking our lives more seriously. But after the transplant, it was cleverness that went out the window and the seriousness that lingered. The hot subject has lost its heat, and now, we find ourselves sitting on the floor asking ourselves, "Why *don't* we get married?"

We follow Beth and the professor's lead, but, unlike them, we don't tell anyone. Not even our closest friends. In the spring, we hop a plane to San Francisco and are married by a female Russian judge in the rotunda of City Hall. It seems like the perfect place to marry, not only because it's the city where we first fell in love, but because when we go to buy our marriage license, a seven-foot-tall drag queen in a red patent dress collects our money and tells us where to sign. I am in awe of her. I can't stop staring at her fake eyelashes and her long cascading curls.

"You are beautiful," I tell her, looking up from two feet below.

"So are you, baby," she says, puckering her lips and kissing the air between us. "Happy wedding day!"

Despite the majestic marble steps and columns, the ambience is not particularly romantic. It is a Monday morning and there is a group of elementary school students touring the building with a docent who leads them up to the grand staircase. They stomp their feet and try to listen for the echo of their voices against the walls. "Hellooooooooo," they call. The sounds come back and make rings around us. They make their way past us and wait for our tiny ceremony to take place. Charlie and I wait and watch as they slowly make their way across the mezzanine, like a gaggle of geese, the stragglers and all, to the other side of the building to stand in the balcony that overlooks the steps, the dome, and the whole first floor below.

Under the stately dome, a Russian judge with dyed red hair and burgundy glasses begins the ceremony but interrupts herself, suddenly curious about her state-issued script: "Do you think that line is from Shakespeare?"

"Uh, no. Maybe the Bible?" I say, curious myself.

"Ha!" she snorts. "How about that?"

She says "Charles O'Doily" instead of "O'Doyle," and Charlie looks at me cross-eyed. The entire scene looks like an awkward dress rehearsal of a cast of understudies who don't quite know their parts. We had finalized Charlie's costume at a vintage store on Haight Street the night before: a brown cowboy shirt with pearlized buttons and dark brown chinos. I had flown to San Francisco with a white, knee-length eyelet dress, collared and belted around the waist, folded in my carry-on. While we waited for our time slot, Charlie went around the corner to a flower shop and bought me a bouquet of bright yellow tulips bound with a thin ribbon. He squeezes my fingers as we face each other to take our vows. I'm not actually sure if we're supposed to say, "I do," or "yes," or something from Shakespeare. But when Natasha the Absentminded Judge finally tells us to kiss, Charlie pulls me close, holding my face in his sweaty palms. As I stand there on my tiptoes, my lips pressed against his, the judge lets out a sigh, and the tour group of young people, who have been watching the entire ceremony in silence from the balcony, explodes in cheers and applause.

My mother is speechless when I tell her on the phone what we have just done. The pause is remarkably long, and I just want to make sure she didn't hang up.

"Hello?" I say.

But the person who answers is not her but my father. "What's wrong with your mother? She looks white," he says. When I tell him the news, he is not quiet at all, but screams with joy. "What news! What news!" he says. "We love you both!"

"Mom does, too?" I ask him.

"Yes, she's just caught off guard. She's happy." Then I hear him whisper to her, "Tell them how happy you are."

She gets on the phone and starts to tell us off in Tagalog just as

Charlie and I turn onto Fulton Street, and I look at him like we're two kids in big trouble. She tells us we're selfish and irresponsible, and just before she hangs up, she says, *"Pag-u-untogin ko ang ullo ninyo!"* Translation: "I'm going to take your heads and bash them together."

"Uh-oh," Charlie says, when she finally hangs up.

"Don't worry," I tell him. "She can't stay mad at us."

We walk up the hill back to our hotel to change before we get dim sum and take a ride around, up past the Golden Gate. We keep making calls, though, enjoying the different reactions we're getting. Charlie's brother cackles into the phone for three minutes straight, unable to contain his laughter. My brother refuses to believe us.

"Is this a joke?" he says. "For real. Tell me the truth."

"No," I tell him.

"I won't believe you until I see the marriage certificate."

Charlie's mother starts crying immediately. We hear nothing but sobbing for several minutes. "Mom?" Charlie says.

"Yes, I'm happy, I'm happy," she says, sniffling between breaths. "Now it's time for grandbabies."

My mother calls us back several hours later. We have already driven up to the coast, hiked a trail, and sat on the beach looking out over the Pacific. I pick up the phone, and she says, with the same singsong tone she usually uses to tease me, "Hello, Mr. and Mrs. O'Doyle."

POOR CHARLIE CAN'T CATCH A BREAK. ON OUR HONEYMOON IN Belize, I stand on the beach in a bikini and push out my belly as far as I can without falling over onto the sand.

"Chaaaaaaarlie," I sing to him.

He looks up at fake-pregnant me, rolls over in his lounge chair, and hides his face in a beach towel. He's just barely been forgiven by our parents for our clandestine wedding, and already his wife is hitting him up for sperm.

Once we get back to Baltimore, we visit our three-year-old niece Genevieve often, as she and her parents live just a few blocks down from our building. Charlie comes home exhausted after a day of tossing her in the air, stumbling over his own feet just to make her squeal, and tickling her from her neck down to her feet. He falls like dead weight on the bed, and I stand over him looking disappointed. "Yeah," I say. "You'd never last a day as a dad."

He pops up on his elbows. "What? I'd make a great dad. I'm offended," he says with a scowl.

"Prove it," I say.

When we circle the issue of having a baby, Charlie doesn't avoid it. He looks me square in the eyes and explains his resistance.

"You're not losing this kidney," he says.

"I don't want to lose it," I tell him.

"Okay," he says, like the conversation is through.

"That's it?" I ask.

"No," he says. "I want a baby, too. If you can find a way to have one without losing this kidney, then the conversation will continue."

I never officially asked my doctors if having a baby was out of the question for me. Despite the envy that grows in me when I see pregnant women walking down the street—their bellies protruding over their toes—and despite this craving I cannot ignore, I know that my health is always precarious, tilting on the edge of a cliff. But at night when Charlie sleeps, I look at him and know that I cannot lose this kidney. I devise ways to get what I want without putting us in danger.

IN A MEETING AT AN EMPTY OFFICE BUILDING ONE WEEKDAY EVE-ning, a woman who appears to be the facilitator has high hair from the Glam Rock era and a harsh orange tan from a bottle. Charlie and I squeeze into narrow office seats between several other fresh-faced young heterosexual couples. As the woman clicks through a slideshow of orphans, all categorized by country, she chooses the saddest faces on which to pause. A toddler walking on a cement floor in Guatemala. A baby girl with the sweetest face from China. It is like watching one of those commercials with Sally Struthers—the babies have wide eyes and are swaddled in blankets that look like they have come from flea markets. It tugs at your pathos until you cough up seventeen cents a day.

"Now, these babies, they are really cute. Just look at those little noses," she says, pointing to a toddler with a high afro. "Ethiopia has been a really easy country for us to get the babies and get their paperwork in order."

Seeing the faces of those beautiful babies makes me want to bring them home right now, but I get a creepy feeling from this woman, who speaks about acquiring the children as if they were merchandise. "I don't know how I felt about her delivery," I tell Charlie as we make our way down the florescent-lit hall.

Charlie says, "It felt like I was being sold a car." He cringes and shakes, as if to get the woman's hard sell off him.

I know what he means. This is different from what we had imagined they'd tell us—stories about the children and what they were like, and how we could open our home to them. But deciding on a country and basing our decision on what the babies look like—it just doesn't feel right.

"So, maybe we should just hold off on this for now?"

"Having a baby?" Charlie asks.

"No, adoption."

"Um, okay."

"We should just see if I can get pregnant."

Then, BOOM! Before he has a chance to agree, Charlie is sitting next to me in a clinic for high-risk obstetrics. The OBGYN is an old man. He is wearing a navy bow tie with bright red squares all over it, but I can't take my eyes off his ears, with their long, low-hanging lobes. The old man wears thick glasses, and he doesn't look up from them. His eyes focus on the folder in his hands, which, among other things, includes a letter from my nephrologist as to the reason we are there.

The doctor doesn't read the words aloud but mumbles through the sentences under his breath, the way people do when they are reading quickly and just trying to find the point of it all. He guides a finger through the lines on the pages as he skims through the information.

"Your medical history is extensive," he says, still not looking up from his desk. "Two transplants."

"Yes, one from my brother, and one from my husband," I say, turning to Charlie.

"Mm-hm," the old man says. When people hear about my medical history, they are usually impressed. But this guy? He acts like I came from central casting. Straitlaced old-timers like this always make me nervous. I'm trying to understand what he sees when he looks over at me. It is difficult to be taken seriously about pregnancy by an aging obstetrician when you look like you're seventeen. I've been known to overcompensate for this insecurity. At the risk of sounding like a loquacious adolescent, I respond succinctly. I refrain from an impulse to smile (I think my smile makes me look younger), and I attempt to keep mature company, though with Charlie's loose-hanging jeans and his holey orange t-shirt, I'm sure this doctor thinks we're both young idiots who want to get pregnant when they know they shouldn't.

"There are risks," he says. "There's small birth weight . . ." —he continues to rattle them off in a sleep-inducing monotone— " . . . pre-eclampsia . . ." and while I'm listening, I'm just waiting for the okay. I am ready to hate him, but his words weigh heavy on me. Especially when he says "loss of the graft," or in other words, "loss of Charlie's kidney." That's the one I hope he'll overlook or the one he might not consider a threat. "All this being said," he finishes, "I can't tell you what to do. I can't tell you to get pregnant or not. But . . . I would not recommend it. A pregnancy probably would not work out well for you." He takes his reading glasses off his face, tosses them to the corner of the desk, and eases back into his chair.

This is not the answer I am hoping for. I came to his office so excited because Charlie was willing to come with me and listen to what the doctor had to say, and this is the bullshit he hears. Now I wish Charlie hadn't come with me, that maybe I could go home and construe this conversation a different way for Charlie, focusing on the part where the doctor says, "I'm not one to tell you what to do." I want to take my hands and cup them over this little man's mouth.

"Your consultation is appreciated," I tell him. The old doctor stands but doesn't move from behind the desk. He waits for us to leave the room. Walking out of his office, I see the young pregnant ladies of Baltimore—the lady with a bulge pushing through her button-down business shirt, the mother already pushing a jog stroller with twin toddlers, a Latina teenager with large hoop earrings the size of her shoulders. Their bellies are round and full, and I try not to hate them.

Charlie holds my hand in the elevator. We stand side by side facing the door. I keep my eyes focused on the row of numbers above, how they darken one by one as we descend. I try to keep from crying.

Charlie hunts for our car in the parking garage, which seems much colder now than it was when we arrived. "I think we're up a level," he says, to cut the silence between us. I trail behind him as he starts up the stairs, and I think, *What does that doctor know?*

"3C or 3D. I can't remember," Charlie says, making a left out of the stairwell.

I want something different. I want him to tell us how to start making plans. To hope for the best, even if we have to plan otherwise. Before I realize it, I am standing behind our car and Charlie is holding the passenger side door open. I look up from staring at the bumper.

"How dare he!" I shout. My voice resonates against the concrete walls and it feels powerful for only a few seconds before it fades into the corners of the garage. Charlie stops and looks around to see if there is anyone else nearby. "I mean, how dare he, right? He doesn't know how it is going to work out."

"Moon, the guy has a pretty good idea. Isn't that why we were there?" Charlie says, walking closer to me cautiously.

"But you never know what can happen. This isn't anybody, right?"

Charlie nods.

"Isn't that what you always say, Charlie? Maybe if we believe something magical can happen, it will."

"He's just looking out for your health," Charlie says. "He's just giving you the facts."

"No, he wasn't looking at the possibilities. The good possibilities. He was only looking at the bad." Charlie knows I'm right. He exhales and his shoulders deflate.

"I know what you mean," he says. "That guy was totally negative. He was like a wall we couldn't penetrate."

I am not crying, but as we stand there, I try to imagine our lives three years from now, a baby toddling between us. One that moves like Charlie, has a defiant look, a stiff chin. Maybe he imagines something similar.

"You want this, huh?"

I nod.

"If you really want this, then maybe we can make it happen."

THE NEXT WEEK, I MAKE AN APPOINTMENT WITH ANOTHER HIGH-risk doctor at a community hospital north of the city that may not have the prestige of the university hospital but has a reputation for its solid obstetrics department. Yes, I admit it: I am shopping around for a second opinion, or a third, until I get the right answer. It seems unethical, like I'm cheating the results of an experiment. The scenario is the same, only this time, the doctor is in scrubs and he smiles when we take our seats in front of his desk. Silver hair and piercing green eyes, he has color in his cheeks and his ear lobes are undoubtedly normal sized. A good sign! Lebanese, maybe, and he moves swiftly like he keeps himself in shape.

"You know, a surrogate would be ideal," he begins, looking at us over his tortoiseshell reading glasses. *Oh, boy, here we go again.* I've decided that this time, no matter how I look or sound, I will be honest with him.

"Yes, but—" I start.

"But you want to get pregnant," he says, smiling. "Yes. I know." Clearly, he's heard about this overwhelming feeling women get as they move into their early thirties, wanting their bodies to experience something more. He has listened to them. "Well, there are risks—you would have to come in once a week so we can check on you and the fetus. The baby might be small; you might be on bed rest for many months to prevent pre-eclampsia. No questions asked."

"Bed rest, I can do," I say, confident that it would be like a vacation.

"We would have to make special arrangements for weekly labs and closer monitoring. But it can be done."

"Have you delivered a baby from a transplanted woman before?" Charlie chimes in with a question that has probably been brewing in his head for a while.

He tells us that he had a patient who had had four kidney transplants and delivered twins. "She was fine; the babies were fine. Now, that's no indication of what your pregnancy will be like," Silver Fox says, looking at me over his glasses. "I'm just saying that it's quite possible that you'll be fine, too."

Quite possible.

DRIVING SOUTH ON CHARLES STREET, THE SUNLIT ROAD BEFORE us is broad and unwrinkled. We're almost home when we pass an apartment window covered with a familiar poster: BELIEVE.

"It's a sign!" I point.

"Literally!" Charlie says. But I know it's an omen; the universe is guiding us. "So, we're doing this?" he asks, drawing in a long, slow inhalation before blowing it out.

I nod.

"Adoption is out?"

"Out!" I yell.

"Well, there are stipulations."

"There are always stipulations."

"You have to do whatever he says. I mean bed rest, and the weekly appointments, we'll have to look at your diet again . . ."

He goes on, his voice fading with the passing landscape. "So, let the procreation begin!" I hear Charlie's announcement, but I'm concentrating on an image slowly coming into focus in my head. It is a baby, sweaty and squirmy, in my arms.

THAT NIGHT, AS WE CLIMB UP TO OUR APARTMENT, I TAKE ON THE staircase in giant, exaggerated leaps without holding on to the banister. "Slow down," Charlie calls. When we get to our floor, a tiny spot of color hangs off the top step. Lying there is a knit cap, striped around the crown with all the colors of the rainbow, small enough to fit around a softball. Earflaps and straps hang from either side of its narrow brim.

Charlie holds it carefully in a nest of his fingers as if it were a bird with a broken wing. Somewhere in this place an infant's little head is cold.

"A sign!" I whisper, as we stand in the hallway and hover over it.

"It must be our neighbor's," Charlie says.

"Can't we keep it?" I ask.

"No, because that would be psycho. I'll bring it back," he says, heading down the dark end of the hall where we rarely venture.

Back in our apartment, I pull the blinds of the living room window up all the way. Outside, Baltimore teems with activity. There are sirens blaring down the alley behind us, and people are in the streets outside a local café. Three weeks ago, I stashed a jumbo bottle of neonatal vitamins in the back drawer of my bureau. When Charlie's not looking, I take two of them into the kitchen, and gulp them down with iced tea.

A few minutes later, Charlie is in the kitchen making himself a sandwich when there is a knock at the door. A woman in a pale cotton dress stands in the hall, and in her arms is a beautiful baby with silky black hair and full, pink lips shiny with drool. "Thanks for dropping off the cap. I just thought you'd want to know who's been keeping you up at night."

"Oh, my god," I tell her. "She's gorgeous." I hold out my hand, but the baby pulls away from me. She digs her face into her mother's chest.

"This is Isabella!"

I stand there trying to put these two in the same family, but their differences are glaring. The baby has café latte skin and dark irises. She has thick everything: legs, head, cheeks, and arms. Our neighbor is pale and blue-eyed. And slim! She doesn't look like someone who's given birth recently.

"Is she—" My words come out quickly, and I'm still trying to form my sentence after they escape my lips. "Did you—"

"Yes," she says, happy to relieve me of my awkward questioning, "we just adopted her. I spent last month in Guatemala getting to know her. And now, she's mine!" She smiles broadly again, and this time I notice her dimples, which strangely now appear to be a trait she shares with her adopted daughter.

Charlie closes the door softly when they leave. "Cute," he says, and goes back to his sandwich. I return to the bedroom. *So much for signs!* I think as I plop myself on the bed, but I don't dare say it aloud for fear the universe, or Charlie, might hear.

Chapter Twelve

COMMENCING on DATES to BE DETERMINED: The STARLING of GREAT IMAGINATION

. . .

I HAVEN'T REALIZED IT UNTIL NOW, BUT CHARLIE AND I HAVE been prepping for the homemaking and parenting stages of our lives since coming to Baltimore. Once our lease is up, we settle on a skinny two-bedroom row house with hardwood floors and ceiling fans. The apartment was feeling too cramped, even with just the two of us. And while the market is filled with newly rehabbed houses, we get our first loan and make our first major investment.

Charlie starts to sweat as we sign the closing papers, and the stuffy old lawyer with the horn-rimmed glasses says to him, "It's just one responsibility after another from here on out."

At first, the place seems like a good size for me and Charlie. But sometimes, when he is upstairs and I am in the kitchen, I can feel the whole floor separating us. We have so little furniture— really just the beastly beige couch—that the floor plan, though skinny, looks spacious and wide. I tell Charlie that there is room to fill, and he nods. I assume we are thinking about the same kind of new occupant—a sleepy one that wears diapers. But Charlie thinks we are talking about someone else, and drives me up the hill to the local SPCA. Charlie's wanted a dog since we were living in Iowa. He always had one growing up, and I think he misses the silent companionship. We are greeted by a wall of sound, happy yelping and dogs bouncing off the high fences of their cages. There is one quiet fellow—a bluetick coonhound with silky black ears that hang below his handsome face. He keeps drawing us back to cage number three with his lonely eyes.

"That little grifter pulled a fast one on us," Charlie says the month after we bring him home. For despite his gentle looks, the hound is a bad boy. His bark, which he kept hidden so well in the kennel, is loud like a foghorn, and it ricochets off the narrow walls of the row house, back and forth, and rings in our ears. The bark might be considered funny or cute if he could only control it. But Bluey has just one volume: *deafening*. And he unleashes that bark at every UPS truck, mailman, bus, cat, skateboard, bicycle, motorcycle, rollerblade, garbage truck, and horse-drawn fruit cart that goes past our front window.

Our quiet little home suddenly becomes a madhouse wherein Bluey is barking and I'm yelling at him to stop while Charlie is chasing him around so he doesn't jump on the windows and click his nails on the glass. Charlie holds our dog down for as long as he can, while, out of breath, he looks up at me and says, "And you want to add someone else to the mix?"

My new nephrologist gives me her blessing about getting pregnant, acting like it's not really an issue at all, and warns me that, in her experience with transplanted women, she finds that they don't usually worry about whether or not they *should* get pregnant. They worry about whether or not they *can* get pregnant. *Another dare*, I think. Clearly these doctors don't know with whom they are dealing.

Charlie's one stipulation is that if we are going to try to get pregnant, we are not going to become slaves to the fertility industry. "Your body doesn't need any more injections or medications or procedures," he says, and I agree. "If we have to go through all that, then let's just assume that it wasn't meant to be."

When I first got on the pill as a young twentysomething, I was amazed by its predictability. The doctors told me I wouldn't get cramps, and I didn't. The doctors told me I'd get my period on the same day of each cycle, and I did. I didn't get pregnant and my breasts did swell while I was on the pill, just like everyone said they would. So I just figured that coming off the pill would be the same: I'd stop taking it and my period would appear. I expected there would be some lag time, but after six months, there is still no sign of my old friend.

During my most recent visit with the doctor, I read in a women's magazine about the benefits of acupuncture to well-being and fertility. After Charlie deems acupuncture not medical enough, I make my way to a small office on the north side of town where there is no receptionist, just rows and rows of oriental herbs on a shelf against the wall.

"My system is whacked," I tell the well-dressed Chinese man in his mid-forties. He wears a neatly pressed collared shirt and matching tie. His accent is sometimes hard to break through, but his friendly demeanor elicits my patience. Right now, he is confused by *my* vernacular. "It's not working," I clarify. At first, I don't tell him that I'm trying to get pregnant, just that I'd like to start getting my period again.

"Oh, yes," he nods.

In a tiny but well-lit exam room, we go over my long, long medical history. As I speak, I occasionally look at the wall above the exam table, where there is a calendar with Chinese characters in red and gold. On the table at which we sit, there is a miniature plastic model of the human body, but instead of pictures depicting the human anatomy, it is marked by little dots in blue and red and cryptic coordinates: TE 23, ST 6. Dr. Cheng sees me concentrating on it and enlightens me: "Meridians," he says. I've been to many a doctor's office, so I know what to expect: how to breathe into the stethoscope when a doctor puts it to my heart or to my back, what my pulse rate should be. But this office is like traveling in a foreign land. Even the examination customs are exotic.

"Okay. Show me your tongue," he says. I open wide, assuming he is looking at my throat.

"Okay. Is very good," he says, nodding as he jerks away from me to face the desk. "A good color." He draws a U shape in his notes to resemble a tongue, and next to it he writes "Red." He pulls out a small velvet pillow from a drawer and asks me to rest my wrist there so he can take my pulse. He presses with two fingers just below my palm, and I assume that he is counting the beats of my heart. He writes something down; it is not a number but a picture of a wavy line.

"Okay, other one," he says, and points to my other wrist. *Wouldn't the pulse be the same?* I think, but apparently not, because this time after he listens, the line he draws has waves that are closer to each other.

He explains that he will work on my spleen, which I assume is, in some mythical way, connected to my ovaries.

Once I am lying on the table, he pins me with the hairlike needles. They are on my arms, on my legs, and sprinkled over my belly. They feel like tiny gnats sitting on the top of my skin.

"Is okay?" he asks, before leaving me in the room. For ninety minutes, I lie perfectly still listening to the Chinese Muzak playing overhead. The warm air coming through the vents and the soft lighting cause me to doze off for a while, but I awake with a jolt. It feels like my body twitched as I slept, strong enough to wake me up. When I ask Dr. Cheng about the sudden movement, he explains that, in that moment, my body became balanced. Oh, how I love this, the different systems of the body becoming perfectly aligned.

"I will give you six more treatments. On the fourth treatment, you will get your period," he says, with such clear vision of the future that it is difficult to doubt him.

I treat my appointments with Dr. Cheng like spa treatments. On Thursday afternoons, I walk into his office, flash him my tongue, hold out my wrists, and nap as still as I can so as not to disrupt the tiny needles he has placed. I wait patiently for that balancing jolt.

On a Friday, the day after my fourth treatment, I wake up in the morning with a familiar cramp in my pelvis, and that afternoon, I see my old friend.

"Now, I want to get pregnant," I tell him on the following Thursday.

He has no questions about whether I should or how it agrees or disagrees with my medical history. Instead he looks at my tongue, checks my pulse, and says, "First thing, you have to think positively. Some women, they think, *Oh, I won't have baby. I'll never have baby.* Not like that. You must think positively!"

"Now you sound like my husband," I tell him, rolling my eyes.

"Your husband is good man?" he asks. "Then he is right.

Think good thoughts. And you must eat a wide variety of foods: meat, fruits, vegetables. But not raw vegetables. Lamb is good. You eat lamb?"

"No, but I will!" I say, hoping that he will not think my enthusiasm is sarcastic.

"Your husband, too."

"Okay, we will!" I say, with the same gusto as before. I gather my keys and my ChapStick from my purse and make plans to go to the store and buy lamb before I go home. "But when will I get pregnant?" I look up, brushing my hair from my face.

I don't know if he doesn't hear me, or if he is choosing deliberately to ignore me, but he leaves the question hanging in the air.

CHARLIE DOESN'T ASK ME ABOUT MY ACUPUNCTURE APPOINTMENTS. At first, I think he doesn't want this as badly as I do, that maybe he's giving our decision a second thought. But sometimes when I wake up in our bed in the mornings, he looks over at me and says, "You think you're pregnant yet?"

He doesn't ask often, but it makes me think that it's in the back of his mind and he doesn't want to talk about it simply because he doesn't want to jinx it.

"Maybe," I tell him each time, trying to stay positive.

WHEN I IMAGINE TELLING CHARLIE ABOUT THE PREGNANCY, IT goes like those television commercials for pregnancy test kits, where the handsome, clean-shaven husband stands next to his glowing wife in their sunlit bathroom, waiting impatiently for the line to turn into a cross. Our experience doesn't go anything like this.

Before he comes back from his morning walk with the dog, I breathe slowly, pacing up and down in front of the bathroom preparing my delivery. I can't think of a way to properly say it, so I decide to use a visual. He is sweaty and worn out, resting on the couch for a second before he gets ready for work. I hold the urine stick in front of him so he can see the lines that make a cross. It takes a long while for him to understand exactly what he is looking at. I realize at that moment that this is probably not the smoothest way to tell my husband that we are pregnant, forgetting of course that he has probably never seen a positive pregnancy test, or any pregnancy test, in his life.

"We're going to have a baby?" he asks, trying to piece together the clues I'm giving him.

"Yup," I say, biting my lip, waiting for the eruption.

There is a pause. A pregnant one. Pun intended—because, yes, it is heavy and bloated and hangs out there waiting to give birth . . . to what? Charlie's forehead beads with sweat, and he looks like he is in a state of shock. He has every right to be. He is about to be a father. We just made a baby together. I stood in the bathroom alone just minutes ago in that same stunned silence.

"Congratulations," he says quite properly. "It's what you've always wanted." He holds out his hand waiting for me to shake it.

Shakes my hand! Like I have just been given a promotion at work, and he is the surprised, but jilted, co-worker. I cannot remember a time when I heard Charlie tripping over his words. But there he stands, paler than usual. I take his hand to shake it, like the graduate who's just been handed her diploma by her principal. And in doing so, I cannot help but laugh. Looks like the sharp-tongued bastard can get rattled! I ignore the fact that he has said this is what *I've* always wanted; I know he couldn't control his reaction. For the rest of the week, I watch as Charlie runs into the banister while walking up the stairs and trips over the dog's leg in the kitchen.

Then one night, while we are sitting on the couch reading, I notice him looking over at me. Then he holds his hand over my belly.

"Feel anything yet?" he asks.

"Charlie, it's only been a week."

"There's someone in there," he says. "That's wild, isn't it?"

"Yeah, it's what I always wanted," I say, smiling devilishly at him.

"You caught me off guard!" he protests. He slinks down into the couch cushion, and looks despairingly up at the ceiling fan. "I know. I'm an idiot." He shrugs his shoulders like a shy little boy. "Just, don't tell anyone about that."

"Yes, Charlie," I say, assuring him. "I'll never tell anyone."

DR. CHENG APPLAUDS WHEN I TELL HIM THE NEWS.

"It's happening! It's happening!" I tell him, looking to him to confirm my disbelief. He says that I shouldn't stop getting treatments, which I don't quite understand since I am pregnant already. *We did it!* I want to say to him.

"Now we will prepare your body for the baby," he says, reminding me that the hard part isn't over. "Your body is still vulnerable. So is this fetus. You must think of your uterus as a house." He holds the tips of his fingers against each other to make an A-frame roof. "You have to make sure that the walls are strong, that the roof does not leak. Otherwise, you would not want to live in it, right?"

I could listen to his poetic imagery all day long. I could stand here and visualize my body as a house now. Not a thing that doesn't work, but a house that protects another being.

As my belly grows bigger, I dive into pregnancy full force. I have been editing a magazine in Baltimore for about a year now, and since I've been pregnant, I sit at my desk rubbing my belly and asking other mothers what I should be doing to prepare.

"Relax," one colleague says. "There will be enough to do when the baby is born."

I take a yoga class with a new-age instructor who has a tight Afro and tattoos around her neck. "Breathe deep," the yogi says. "Breathe the good air into your womb."

I start keeping a journal, writing down what foods I am eating, what new sensations I feel. It seems now like I have influence over how this pregnancy will turn out, like if I am determined to make it work out, it will.

It's the books I'm reading about pregnancy that aren't working out so well for me.

"Bleeding nipples? Misplaced placenta?" I read to Charlie aloud in bed. I grab my breasts and hold my belly. Charlie covers his ears with his hands.

"Don't read ahead!" my officemate tells me when I pull out *What to Expect When You're Expecting* from my backpack. "My friend read ahead and her husband found her in the nursery crying hysterically with fear! She was only in her second trimester."

"So much can go wrong," I tell my mother on the phone one day, summing up what these books are trying to tell me.

"Don't worry so much," she says, waiting to drop more of her superstition on me. "Your worry will make your baby into a worried person." This is the last thing I want. Imagine Charlie with a neurotic kid, a kid who is worried about his head splitting open as Charlie tosses him in the air.

CHARLIE STARTS A JOB AT AN EDUCATIONAL COMPANY WHERE the hours are reasonable and the pay is better. He stands at the top of the steps and looks at every room in the house, planning how to begin to make repairs. He escapes to these quiet, thoughtful moments that have little to do with what's happening inside my body now, and more to do with what will happen after the baby is born.

But then one night, as we are sitting on the couch eating ice cream from the carton, he says, "It'll be a boy. I know it. We'll call him Hawthorne."

"Ugh, too nineteeth-century-early-American-novel-ish."

"Henry," he says, scooping out another spoonful of dulce de leche.

"Kind of the same thing," I tell him.

AT MY MONTH-THREE SONOGRAM, I AM IN A WAITING ROOM. When the nurse calls me in, she holds open the exam room door and says, "Is there anyone with you?"

"Sadly, no," I say. This is one of the moments when I wish Charlie were here—the moment when we find out the sex of our baby. I don't think Charlie cares too much for milestones, though. He uses the excuse that he needs to save up vacation days for when the baby is born. Still, it is difficult to feel so excited all by myself.

The ultrasound room is womblike—dimly lit, warm. If I were

not lying down, I would probably pass out from the heat. I swaddle myself in the white sheets the nurse gives me. The technician runs a bead of cold gel just below my belly button. She checks a few things on the screen.

"Would you like to know what you're going to have?" she says.

"Yes."

"Care to guess?" she asks, looking at the screen, but giving no clues in her smile.

"Boy!" I say, waiting for her to point out a little penis on the screen. A boy, I think. With curly, dark brown hair. A boy, with Charlie's charm. He is in there being rambunctious and smart, athletic and fast, swimming around my uterus as if it were a lap pool.

"How about a girl?"

I turn my head to look at the screen, and there she is. A blurry kernel of popcorn. A girl. Her heart is a flicker; it's a strobe light illuminating the entire screen.

At home, I jump on Charlie as he steps in the door. "A girl!" I say.

Again in shock, the poor boy makes his way slowly to the couch and sinks into the cushion with all his weight.

"Are you excited?"

"Yeah, yeah," he says, smiling. "But what am I going to do with a girl?"

My head snaps back at his remark; it feels like a knock to the nose.

"What?" he sits up and asks. "What did I say? Why are you crying?"

I don't realize I am crying until he says so. I put my hands to my face, and sure enough, they are wet with tears.

"It's the hormones," I say, shaking my head. But then: "No. Wait, why do you have to say it like that?"

"Uh," he says, angry with himself, "I'm saying all the wrong things! I meant to say, 'What's a girl gonna do with me?' How am I going to know what she wants? How am I going to make her stop crying? And how am I going to help you through this? What am I supposed to do? I'm already screwing it up."

I listen to him unload, and I grab his hand.

"You can do this, Charlie," I tell him. "I really believe you can."

AS SOON AS WE TELL OUR PARENTS THAT WE'RE HAVING A GIRL, Charlie's mother begins sneaking in a suggestion here and there every time we see her. "Louise," she says. "Or Laura." And once, "Maureen, maybe." The way she enunciates her syllables makes the names sound particularly melodic. They are storybook names for girls with banana curls and petticoats. I try to picture a Louise coming out of my body, and the image seems alien and surreal. Or maybe I am the alien, giving birth to someone completely unlike me.

I want a name that might show off her ethnicity, something that will match her (hopefully) brown skin and dark eyes. Nothing too long. Nothing ending with a soft "a" sound or, especially, a long "e" lest the girl eventually change the spelling of her name so it ends with the letter "i" which, during her teenage notewriting years, she will inevitably dot with a puffy heart. We shall prevent this at all costs.

Charlie sends me emails from work with only a name written in the subject line. All his suggestions emphasize the "u" sound: *Beulah, Lula, Maru.* When I read them out loud at my desk, I pucker my lips and passersby must think I'm trying to kiss the screen. I write him back: "These make our daughter sound like she's a featured performer in the circus. *And now, ladies and gentle-*

men, if you'll please turn your attention to the tightrope to witness the feats of The Amazing Tululah O'Doyle."

"What's wrong with that?" he writes back.

I shoot his suggestions down like soda cans on a fence.

One day, while sitting at my desk at work, I hear the familiar voice of a woman on the radio, one who always sounds like she is being mowed down slowly by a tank. "I'll be your mirror," Nico moans, "reflect what you are, in case you don't know." And when I take away the sound of her voice and the image of the tall, blonde German model on heroin, I see her name in print—two little cute syllables for one cute little girl.

In early February, when I'm five months pregnant, Maggie, another friend from Iowa, emails me to congratulate me on the pregnancy. I know that she's been trying to get pregnant for months, and I think that it is selfless of her to be so happy for me. She also tells me that she read an article in the *New York Times* about a woman who found her kidney donor on the Internet. She writes that she is "seriously considering being a donor."

"For whom?" I wonder.

"For someone who needs a kidney. Anyone," she writes.

"We need more people like you in the world," I write her. And I mean it. Maggie, with her powerhouse body and adventurous attitude, would be a perfect donor. I could see her giving up her kidney to a stranger for the sheer joy of knowing that she could help someone. But in her email, she reminds me that none of the insemination efforts she and her wife have been trying have worked. She'd probably have to donate before her next insemination.

But I can't imagine her trying to get pregnant after she'd had an operation to remove her kidney. Then what? Have a baby on one kidney?

"Yeah," she writes, "but I wouldn't have the complications that you do. I would have one kidney, but my overall health would be good."

I want to be encouraging, but I don't want to tell her something that might put her in the same situation that I am in. Not that I've been alerted to any problems yet, but the worry of what could happen sits in the back of my mind. This baby may not make it to full term. Neither might I.

"Just wait for now," I tell Maggie, wanting her to consider it more carefully. "Just look into it, but don't do anything yet."

"MOTHERHOOD IS FULL OF CHOICES," VIOLET CALLS FROM VEGAS to tell me. As she talks, the one-year-old in her arms coos into the phone. "Every day is like: feed her this or that? Give her milk now or later? Hat or no hat? Put her in the crib or keep her in bed?"

"Sounds exhausting," I say.

"I'm just tired of having to think every scenario through, you know? I'm surprised those little dilemmas aren't bothering you already."

"Should they?"

"Well, what are you going to do after maternity leave? Are you going back to work? Full-time or part-time? Are you getting a nann—"

"Stop!" I tell her. "No more!"

"No," she corrects me before hanging up. "Plenty more."

When I hang up the office phone, I turn to Kristi and I say, "Think the boss would let me go part-time after the baby's born?"

She answers without looking away from her computer screen, "Eh. Well, no. I don't know. Then she'll have to cover all that editing herself. She might as well hire someone new."

"But why would I have this baby if I'm not going to spend every waking minute with her?"

"Uh," Kristi says, "are you sure that wouldn't drive you insane? It would make me crazy."

I just can't imagine this little thing driving me crazy if she's not even here yet.

At around five months, I ask my mother, "Shouldn't she be kicking by now?"

"You'll know when the baby kicks," my mother says. "Imagine that you've got a little bird in your hand, and it's moving around on your palm, pecking around your fingers." She raises up her closed fist and smiles as if she has something inside it. This is the gentlest I've ever known my mother to be—she opens her hand slowly, and though nothing is inside, she peeks behind her fingers and smiles coyly into her palm.

Every week, the Silver Fox measures my belly as I lie back on his exam table. And every week, I have new questions for him. This week I ask him how I will deliver.

"I want to push," I tell him. Over the years, all those movies with pregnant women pushing and screaming while yelling at their husbands has become the way I imagine birth to be: loud, raw, and painful.

"There is no reason why you wouldn't be able to deliver vaginally. If everything goes well with the pregnancy, the kidneys shouldn't be a problem. They will not be in the way of the birth canal." He pulls a measuring tape across my belly to assess its growth, then stops and rolls the tape back up in his hand to make sure we're clear on one thing:

"But if something happens, and I tell you that you'll need a C-section, then you will have a C-section. That is not up for debate." He pulls the measuring tape over me again, and I laugh when I look down and cannot see my feet.

ONE NIGHT, I DREAM THAT I AM STANDING AT THE TOP OF THE stairs in our tiny row house with my bare feet on the hardwood floor. I peer down the steps and, just under the living room window, there is a bird. It is tiny and pale blue, with furry white wings, and it is busy picking at a floorboard in the living room. When I see it, I immediately yell for Charlie: "Charlie! Charlie!" I scream. "Come quick! There's a bird in the house. There is a bird in the house!" Charlie slides past me in his socks and comes sweeping down the steps in his pajamas. He swings around the banister and stops in front of the little bird. It looks up at him, too frightened to move. Charlie cups it in his hands and holds it up for me to see. I peer at it from a safe distance.

When I tell my mother about my weird dream, she giggles and shakes her head. *"Anak,"* she says, "that bird in your dream is your baby."

The dream haunts me for days, or rather, my reaction does. It plays over and over in my head. The scream that came out of me when I saw that bird. And here's what bothers me most: I can't figure out if I was calling out in worry or delight or utter terror.

Chapter Thirteen

The WOMAN
WHO SWALLOWS FIRE
and EXHALES ANGELS

• • •

I AM NOT WELL-VERSED IN CHILI COOK-OFF ETIQUETTE, SO I JUST stand in a corner counting the bowls in other people's hands. There are three conference tables laid out end to end in the fourth-floor hallway of my office. I have finished six bowls of chili, and I could have eaten seven or eight. The employees have been asked to try all of them before submitting their votes. I am the only one in the office willing to admit that this is nearly impossible. But by the fifth one, I'm certain I know which one my winner will be. The one with the chocolate in it. The base is thick and dark, and the chocolate gives richness to the tomatoes. There were two I sampled that were hot, hot, hot; afterward, the little bird inside me pushed hard against my uterine wall. She stretched her legs gradually into my ribs after I spooned in the one with chocolate, so I knew I had a winner.

I notice on the drive to work that the steering wheel is slowly inching its way closer and closer to me. I admit that I am feeling particularly loaded today, thick around my ankles and around my face.

Over the weekend, I was worried about my face, which seemed particularly thick in the mirror. "Well, your name *is* Moonface, right?" Charlie'd said. Looking in the mirror, I was unsure if I was worrying too much. I went for a blood test first thing on Monday morning just to be sure.

It is April and the sun comes through the windows and makes large yellow squares on the patterned carpet. A co-worker sits down next to me with a bowl of chili (not my pick). "So, how much longer you got?"

"Two months. Can you believe it?" I raise my pant leg to show him my elephant-like ankles.

"Man," a woman beside us interjects, "don't you wish you could just get the darn thing over with? I was pregnant with my first two all through summer, and my thighs were so thick it felt like they were glued together the whole time."

"June," I say, trying desperately to get that image out of my head. "But I'm not complaining."

If I do say so myself, pregnancy has changed me. I've lived my whole life in a body that looks like it belongs to a prepubescent boy. Charlie and I even used to have a character based on it. I'd stuff my hair into a baseball cap, put on a flannel button-down and jeans, and walk around smacking gum and throwing a baseball into a mitt. "Hey, Ricky," Charlie used to call me as we walked beside each other down the street. It was funny to us for a while until Charlie started worrying that people in the neighborhood would think he was a pedophile.

But now, that gangly body has been replaced by hips I can rest my arms on and breasts that actually protrude. And with a belly that has just begun to fill out my maternity jeans, there's no denying that I am a woman. I can see other people noticing it, too. They look at me like they are watching something beautiful happen, like they're standing behind a street artist as he paints a view of the city. They can't take their eyes away.

Someone is taking pictures for the company website, and as she passes by me, she says, "Wait! I've got to take a picture of the pregnant woman!" So I stand up for her, with my belly in full effect, holding my number-one chili pick.

With my stomach full, I take a slow duck walk back to my desk to find my voicemail light flickering. There are two messages. The first is from my nephrologist, who tells me that my lab results indicate that I have pre-eclampsia, and with my blood pressure so high, the baby's health is in danger. I should come into the hospital now, she says. The second call is from the Silver Fox, who says the same thing, but with urgency. "I will not be there when you arrive, but my partner will be waiting for you," he says. "This is what I talked about. Go now."

I hang up the phone. I reach for my belly, thinking that I should be able to feel a heartbeat or something, right? Even though I haven't been able to feel one through this whole pregnancy without my doctor holding one of those microphones to my stomach. I should be able to feel her, right? Or at least she should be able to tell me she's all right.

Melissa, my boss, is a mother of two, and I think only a mother can drive me to the hospital the way she does, her wheels screeching as she slides under the LABOR AND DELIVERY entrance sign, a *Dukes of Hazzard* moment if ever I had been in one. She goes from running a tractor-trailer off of I-83 with her lightning-fast Honda to gently putting a comforting hand on my back as she walks me to the front desk. Her heels click and clack in the lobby, and when a receptionist tells me they've been waiting for me, Melissa holds my hand for several seconds before click-clacking away. Now it's just a matter of getting Charlie there, too. This morning he rode his bike to work, and the nurses are telling me that Charlie should come now, find a way to get from downtown to beyond the county line within the hour. "He should ditch the bike," she says.

I call Charlie at work and I tell him what is happening, and he answers with a series of breathless "okays," as if he's going to jump off the phone call and into a race. That's exactly what this feels like: a race. How to get everyone in place—the delivery team, Charlie, and the baby—all in the same room before it's too late.

A female doctor, who is Silver Fox's partner and resembles Carrie Fisher with warm brown eyes, sits on a couch in my hospital room and says, "I think you're going to deliver this baby before Friday." It is Wednesday, eleven weeks before the baby's due date. I keep trying to remember in the books I've read what hasn't yet formed. Lungs? Fingers? Will my baby have feet? The lady doctor goes through my chart and rereads my history. "Two transplants," she says. "You're not going to make this easy for me. Order another set of labs for her," she says to the nurse.

Fifteen minutes later Princess Leia says that I will probably deliver tonight. Fifteen minutes after that, she tells me I will probably deliver within the hour and *where the hell is my husband?*

It is too fast to worry about the baby or me. Clearly these people know what they are doing—more than I know what is happening to me. As they run the ultrasound probe over me again, I give Charlie another try on his cell phone, though I am unsure he knows completely how to use it, since he was a self-proclaimed Luddite before I told him he needed to get a cell phone for this pregnancy. *Freakin' Luddites*, I think now. *Where is he?* I'm beginning to sense the urgency of the situation as the doctor orders a test to examine the physical health of the baby.

I'm chewing on the edge of the bed sheet, gnawing over all my worries, when a nurse comes in and says, "How's your pubic hair situation?"

And I know I should be thinking something serious right then. But I look at her holding the electric razor and I just bust out laughing and so does she. *Is this for real?* Maybe it isn't as bad as I think. Just then, my husband comes in, running through the threshold as if he had just finished a marathon, his pale face now red and sweaty.

"Charlie!" I say, throwing my arms open toward him.

"You've got to go get ready," says the nurse and, before he has a chance to speak, she spins him around by his shoulders and says, "Go prep!"

"Okay!" Charlie says, running out the door.

THE NEXT TIME I SEE CHARLIE, MY PUBIC HAIRS ARE SHAVED AND Charlie is in a soufflé-like yellow hat and yellow gown, and he's sitting on a stool next to my head.

The anesthesiologist introduces himself while I am splayed out on the operating table being prepped for the C-section. During pleasantries and introductions, we discover that I spent part of my childhood in the same Pennsylvania town where his wife grew up. As we wait for the doctor to arrive, he starts naming people I might know. I know none of them. I'm thinking he got the town name wrong.

"Tina Beckman," he says.

"No, I don't think so."

"John Beckman?"

"Where's the doctor?" I ask nervously, wanting to get the surgery going.

"She's coming," the anesthesiologist assures me.

Charlie sits on a stool staring up at a wall of medical supplies: gauze, long plastic tubes, steely scissors. He rubs my forearm and mumbles to himself, "I will not look past the curtain; I do not want to look past the curtain." His brother has already taught him how to handle a C-section so he will not faint: "Don't look past the curtain," Wes drilled into him. "Do not stand up from the stool."

When Princess Leia arrives, she's ready to operate. She holds a scalpel up in the air, and I can see the sharp end peeking out just above the curtain. She says, "Okay, here we go," and dives in like I'm a salad.

"Do you know Ellen Casperato?" the anesthesiologist says, as he looks at the monitor over my head.

"No."

"Where did you say you went to high school?" Despite his preoccupation with our finding a common acquaintance, he seems to be doing his job, because I don't feel a thing as Princess Leia dictates to her team.

"Okay, we're gonna get her now," she says.

Charlie and I lock eyes; he's staring deeply at me, sending me telepathic signals and saying everything is going okay. The anesthesiologist stops his name game for a second and leans down close to Charlie: "Um, sir, perhaps you'll want to look up now.

Your baby girl is being born." Charlie cranes his head above the curtain, lifting his body only a few inches off the stool. He is silent. The room is silent. I am just waiting to hear the cry. One cry. One sound. Let me hear that bird. I can't see anything beyond the curtain, no matter how much I lift my head.

"Oh, dear! Look at her," Charlie calls out.

"What?" I ask. "How is she?"

Another nurse says, "Oh, my."

"What?" I say. I still don't hear a cry. There is the ruffling of paper linens. There is metal clanging against metal.

Charlie lets go of my hand, bounds off his stool, and follows a nurse who is carrying our baby to a corner on the other side of the room.

"Charlie? Where is she?" I call out.

"We're just giving her some tests, Mrs. O'Doyle," a male voice beyond the curtain says.

From the corner, Charlie begins giving me the play-by-play. Though I can't see him—I can't see anyone—I can tell by his voice that he is smiling. "Oh, she's kicking. Oh, look at her arms. She's a knockout, Moonface."

Then: "Waaaaaaaah!"

"Oh! She's yelling!" he screeches, his giddiness rising up over the blue curtain. "Oh, she's pissed, Moonface, she's pissed!"

"Waah! Waah!"

"She's good!" a doctor from the corner says.

"She passes!" Charlie says.

Another doctor brings her near my head, and I see her for the first time. She is brilliant. A loud, crying baby doll, annoyed by the bright lights. She is a tiny, dark bundle with shiny skin, an eggplant enveloped in a pink and blue blanket. I give a kiss on the littlest nose I have ever seen.

"She'll be upstairs in the NICU when you're ready," he says, and they take her up to the Neonatal Intensive Care Unit.

Charlie tries to inhale deeply but clenches his chest and wheezes. He wipes the sweat off his brow with his sleeve. "Whew!" he says, "Whew!" He sits down again and grabs my hand.

Princess Leia and her staff close me up. I can't move anything but my arms, but as I lie there, I think that if I try hard enough, I can get up from this table all by myself and I can go to my baby before she opens her eyes and spots someone else while she's looking for me.

Chapter Fourteen

The LEARNED BIRD
and the BRIEF RETURN
of the DISAPPEARING BEAR

· · ·

SHE IS JUST LIKE THE BIRD IN THE DREAM, WITH HER SOFT SKIN over the smallest bones, her lashless eyelids. My baby's hair is a luscious black. Damp with sweat and waxed against her delicate skull, it emerges from the center in a perfect swirl. And what movements she makes already, at two days old, at two pounds! She drops her jaw open in slow motion like remote-controlled dinosaurs in the movies. She sticks out her tongue to pesky onlookers. She sculpts imaginary clay with her fingers, twisting and turning her hands with deliberate ease.

I thought it would come naturally, but when I go to hold her or touch her in her isolette, the plastic enclosed crib that keeps her warm, I don't know what to do. One of the neonatal nurses, a woman who is younger than I am but surprisingly maternal, shows me how to touch my preemie: "Put a hand on her back and keep it still. If you move it back and forth across her body, it's too startling for her," she says.

Holding her is even more awkward. She's so small, I'm afraid that she will slip through my arms. "Put her head against your chest, so she can feel your heart beating. It reminds her of the womb," she says.

Charlie, whom I thought might be afraid of her tiny frame, does not miss his opportunity to hold her.

"My turn," he says, after I have her for most of that evening. He pulls up one of the NICU rocking chairs and sings her an old folk song. He sings of an ocean full of storms, and a heaven that may not exist. "The world may lose its motion, love," he sings, "if I prove false to thee." Every time she stirs, he stops, holding his hand like a cap on the top of her head to reassure her. And there they sit—Charlie O'Doyle and his little bird, rocking the night away.

When Charlie fills out the application for the birth certificate, he writes the name we've decided on: Nico Carmen. It rings off his tongue when he says it. But when I see her, that name does not yet spring easily from my lips. Maybe because I've been afraid to utter it for so long, thinking that calling out her name before she was born might jinx her. When I look at her now in the flesh, I keep thinking of the baby bird Charlie held in my dream. "She's Birdie," I tell Charlie.

Over the next few days, I should be resting and recovering after all the excitement of the delivery, but I can't stand being away from Birdie for too long. Charlie wheels me up to her during the day and we take turns rocking her in her chair, brushing our fingers against her face. Just after visiting hours are over, or even in the middle of the night, I walk up to the NICU myself in a robe and slippers just to hold her and to feel her head against my chest. She is tethered to her isolette by narrow tubes—a feed tube that goes through her nose, a tube that helps her breathe, and the tiniest blood pressure cuff I have ever seen that wraps around her leg. I cradle her in my arms, and we sit in the subdued light of the ward.

"Your baby is so beautiful!" the Silver Fox says when he comes into my room one morning. His mild, exotic cologne fills the air. "And she seems to be progressing nicely, no?"

He asks to see my wound, and I hold my gown up to my chin. In order to avoid running into the transplanted kidneys that flank my uterus, Princess Leia made a vertical C-section cut instead of the usual horizontal. Underneath some bloody gauze, there is a straight line from my belly button down to my pelvis.

"Hurt?" Silver Fox says as he presses around the outsides of my midriff, which is still bloated from the pregnancy and the surgery.

"No," I say. "I can barely feel the wound at all."

"Now, your creatinine is still high," he says, "but that will take a few days to come down." He nods his head and taps my leg lightly, dismissing any worry I might have. Not that I am too worried to begin with. The delivery was a circus, and for a while I didn't think we would make it. But now that the little bird is breathing and moving around outside of me, I know that everything is going to work out.

One night, on my way to the NICU, a nurse from my ward stops me in the hall and asks me if I want a wheelchair. I tell her I'll walk, but she insists that I use the chair, so I indulge her and relax as she pushes me upstairs. It's sometime past midnight when I put Birdie back in her isolette, but I don't bother to call the nurse for the return ride. As I make my way out of the NICU toward the elevator, the hall suddenly narrows and dark bubbles form around my line of vision. I feel faint and grab at the walls, feeling my way slowly back to my room.

"Are you all right?" the same nurse asks, as she rushes into my room and helps me into bed.

"I just got lightheaded for a second," I tell her.

"It's no wonder," she says, throwing her hands in the air. "Your hematocrit is low. You're anemic. I'm surprised you have the energy to walk."

The anemia doesn't get better. It's so bad that the doctor orders me to have two blood transfusions, hoping that they will give my red blood cells a boost. I should be feeling tired and weak, but, at times, I feel like I am ready to run up to Birdie's bed and talk to her all night.

But my red blood cells don't pick up, and neither does my kidney function, as the Silver Fox had predicted. It creeps up to 2.2, which causes him to worry, so by that afternoon, a suited, clean-shaven nephrologist who seems more like a politician than a doctor looks over my complicated chart.

"I'm worried," he says, looking up at me. And suddenly I am, too. "Your kidney is not coming back up to speed as quickly as we had hoped." He suggests that I go back to the university hospital to get a biopsy done to see what's happening with the kidney, since there are no doctors who specialize in transplants here, and they don't really have the facilities to accommodate my complicated case. His plan seems prudent, but that would require my leaving Birdie at this hospital and getting admitted to the big one all the way downtown.

"It's only for a little while," the nephrologist says when he sees my pout.

"Trust me. You don't want to get a kidney biopsy here."

ALL THE SAME, THESE FIRST FEW DAYS AFTER SHE IS BORN, I AM so concerned with Birdie's growth and making sure all her parts are there and working that I almost forget about my own health. I keep thinking that as long as she is healthy, despite being born premature, everything else will fall into place, that my health will follow.

I tell Charlie that I know the kidney will come back, and he agrees, but it's being away from Birdie that hurts the most.

"Can we move her there with you?" he asks, which is an option, but she is getting such good care from the nurses at this smaller NICU. At the university hospital, she might get lost among all the special cases. Besides, I tell him, I'm afraid she is not yet ready to go out into the big world of roads, bikes, and trucks. "You're right," he says. "It's scary out there."

THE NIGHT BEFORE I'M RELEASED, CHARLIE AND I GO UP TO THE NICU to tell Birdie that I am leaving. Her tiny back is turned to us when we get there, as if she knows what is happening and is not pleased. Charlie and I watch as the nurses check on her, feeling through the armholes of the isolette to touch her. I wait patiently as they work on her.

Then I hold her on my lap as I sit in a rocking chair, her sweaty face stuck to my chest like a decal, and I tell Charlie that I don't think I could bear the idea of not being able to hold her.

"Won't she be looking for me?" I ask him.

"Yes," he says, "she probably will. But I'll tell her where you are. It's only for a few days, until the kidney kicks back in. Think of it like you're the mama bear and you've got to leave the cave and forage for food. It's not just for your health; it's for hers, too."

"I don't know," I tell him. My heart feels like it's being stretched.

"She'll be waiting here after you take care of yourself. You don't want her to have a sick mom."

"What if she thinks someone else is her mother?" I tell him. I don't want anyone holding her but him and the nurses.

The next morning, as I say goodbye to her, a white note is taped to the cover of her isolette. "Only Mommy and Daddy can hold me. Thank you, Nico xoxo." It's written in black Sharpie. I notice the softly rounded o's, and I think, *yes, her handwriting would have softly rounded o's.* Just like her eyes and the tips of her tiny toes, and her mouth when she opens it. I concentrate on all these parts of her body and burn their images into my memory before I leave.

Chapter Fifteen

A VERY SPECIAL DRAMATIC PERFORMANCE: The WORST MOTHER'S DAY in the HISTORY of the WORLD

• • •

Birdie was born in the middle of April, two months before she was supposed to arrive. And though our time in the hospital together was brief, I insist on trying to connect with her. I sit in my hospital room at night and try to send my vibes to her from all the way across town. They snake past the ghetto that surrounds the hospital where I stay, up 83 North, slowly along North Charles Street, and up the serpentine hill to the hospital where she is, straight into her crib. I don't know how much she senses these vibes, but I send them as best I can, at night, alone.

Charlie insists on keeping us connected, too. He videotapes her every night so I can see how she has grown. He records my voice on a small tape recorder and plays it to her as she sleeps. He tells me he has taken one of my shirts from home and has stuffed it around the edges of her crib so she can smell me there with her, so she knows who I am again. How sad, I think, for a child to need such tactics to recognize her mother. How sad for Charlie, too, whose schedule has been complicated by my unfortunate separation from Birdie. He is still working full-time amid all this, walking the dog in the mornings before riding to work downtown. Then he comes to see me at lunchtime with a new video of Birdie, goes back to work, walks the dog, then spends the evening holding Birdie against his chest and filming more footage of her. I live for those videos. I lift myself upright in bed and beg him for details about the girl on those days when he pops in to see me with sandwiches or with some lunch—what is she wearing? How much did she eat? How much does she weigh today?

Our visits are usually interrupted by one of the nurses checking in. "How would you rate your pain today?" she asks. With a quick survey of my body, I tell her, "A one."

"So nothing for pain?"

"Not right now."

"Use the call button if you need me."

"What is wrong with you?" Charlie whispers to me just as she closes the door behind her.

"What?"

"You should never refuse pain meds." Charlie and I have been known to enjoy the occasional pain medications, but only after medical procedures. Sometimes, we try to space out the prescriptions for days so that we can have a few to relax even after there is no pain. Innocent outlaws, we are. Or not even.

"I'm trying to get out of here. They're not going to let me out of here if they still think I'm in pain."

THE BIOPSY SHOWS THAT MY KIDNEY IS SUFFERING FROM AN ACUTE rejection, most likely caused by the pregnancy. "This is a good thing!" the attending doctor, a tall and imposing figure with dark hair and smart-looking neckties, says as he makes rounds one morning, bringing a whole class of young students with him. They circle my bed and nod in agreement. "That means it's reversible!" They want to start me on a course of Thymoglobulin, a drug to help fight the rejection.

"How long will it take?" I ask them.

"At least a week, maybe two," the attending doctor says.

"I have a baby to go home to," I remind them.

I pull him aside and make a plea after the students leave: *I can't lose this kidney.*

"It's special, you know," I tell him. "It's from my husband."

"You won't," he says. I don't really feel like I will, especially after they find that the rejection is acute. But I feel like I should tell them that I won't give it up. Just so they know.

IT'S THE DAY BEFORE MOTHER'S DAY. MY MOTHER, WHO HAS BEEN here since the day after Birdie was born, cannot stand the idea of my being away from my girl. She approaches one of my doctors and asks if she could kindly sneak me out of the hospital for a few hours on Sunday. "She needs to see her baby," she pleads in the hallway while doctors make their rounds. A short Asian resident with a slight lisp tells her he'll grant me a pass for a few hours to spend with her on Mother's Day. But just a few hours.

I was so afraid for Birdie when she was born. What could she do at two pounds? Did I bring her into this world at a disadvantage? I was afraid she wouldn't be healthy enough to make her milestones, that she would lag behind because of her prematurity. I never thought that I would be the one missing out on her important moments. Or mine. Or ours together. As selfish as it sounds, I just didn't think that they would go on without me: her first bottle feeding, her first time taking a bath. I didn't want to think about her first Mother's Day without my being there.

"I've got to get out of here," I tell Charlie. "Because I am really afraid of missing everything. All of it. Her life."

"Don't worry," he says. "You'll see her tomorrow. The two of you can catch up then."

On Sunday morning, my mother arrives early and washes my hair. She brings me a fresh shirt and pants that are easy to slip into. I'm just about ready when a nurse comes in to take my vitals. She looks at the thermometer and shakes her head, and I know immediately that my temperature is high and that I'm not going anywhere. I feel terrible for that small Asian doctor with a lisp, for he is the one who comes in to tell me the news. And he is the one who gets the evil looks from my mother and me—the ones that must bore into his soul like railroad spikes.

"*Permission denied!*" I tell Charlie over the phone, trying to sound authoritative and cruel, trying desperately to laugh through it. But Charlie knows.

"Oh, baby," he says, and when he does, the tears come flooding out, and I can barely respond to him on the phone. I can only eke out frustrating grunts and deep inhalations. "I'll be there as soon as I can," he says.

I beg my mother to leave so she can be with Birdie since I can't. But I just want to be by myself. A heavyset nurse hears me sobbing from the hall and stands silently in the doorway. She comes into my room smelling like she's just come back from a smoke break and pretends to be checking the monitors above my bed.

"Are you in a lot of pain?" she asks.

I nod. "It's my baby," I tell her. "She's so far away." Inhaling deeply, I hoist myself upright and try to find my composure.

"How would you rate your pain on a scale of one to ten?"

"Ten," I say, my nose runny and snotty. I pull the sheet up from my chest.

"Okay," she says, "let's see if the doctors have ordered anything for the pain."

It is the worst pain I have ever felt. It hurts. It hurts all over. It hurts to breathe, like someone is constricting my throat. What is this pain and where does it come from? It feels like someone has taken away part of me or taken away my skin so that everything I touch—the bed, the pillow, even the air—makes my body hurt.

When the nurse comes back, she has an order of Dilaudid in a syringe.

"Just relax," she says, pushing the needle through my IV. Instantly, I feel the medicine rush over my shoulders, making them relax and fall. The calm radiates through my body. It is relief, like I have entered a different world, a different day than this one.

"Were you crying?" Charlie says when he comes in. I don't even know he's there until he speaks.

I lift up slowly to see him and think I am slurring my speech when I say, "Yeah, but I feel better. The nurse gave me a shot."

"Was your stomach hurting?"

"Yeah, duuuude," I say. I think I am smiling.

Charlie laughs. "All right, girl," he says, realizing the state I'm in. "Take it easy. I'll be right here." He sits back and eases into the chair.

Chapter Sixteen

MOONFACE EXHIBITS HER DEATH-DEFYING TOLERANCE for PAIN WHILE in the COMPANY of a TAIL-CHASING DOG

. . .

BIRDIE KEEPS GETTING BETTER. MY PARENTS, IN-LAWS, AND Charlie all report that our little bird continues to grow, giving the doctors nothing remarkable to discuss. Her isolette is slowly being stripped of the various apparatuses that once crowded it: the glaring bilirubin lights, the mask that covered her face and helped her breathe, and a feed tube, which stayed in surprisingly long despite her many attempts to tear it out. She is free of all of them.

"You just ought to see her, Moonface. She is a feisty one," Charlie says, his whole body abuzz as he speaks. He shows me a video of a NICU nurse getting her ready for a bath. Birdie has a petite frame and scrawny arms, but she doesn't seem to know it. She hangs on with her little monkey hands to the top lip of the isolette as the nurse tries to take her out. She cries like a hungry cat as she feels the cold air outside her protective synthetic womb.

"She is three pounds now!" Charlie says, pointing to her wriggly body on the screen. "An ounce since last week!"

• • •

As the Little Bird is gaining her strength, I seem to be losing mine.

I am putting on weight, too, but not the good kind. I am already twenty pounds heavier from the pregnancy, but since my kidney isn't functioning and can't filter out the wastes normally, I am holding fluid under my skin. It feels like an inner tube full of water hangs around my hips. My legs are heavy, making it difficult to swing them over the side of the bed and go for a walk. The poor phlebotomists who have to draw my blood every day spend most of the morning pushing the thick skin around my arms, looking for a vein.

The doctors—all of those who have been following my case—decide that they will put me on dialysis, hoping that getting some fluid off my body will jumpstart the kidney. But I resist the notion every time they bring it up because dialysis has always been an end point for me, and I interpret starting dialysis as pronouncing Charlie's kidney dead.

"No, it's only temporary. It's not forever, just for now, or for a while, you know," says one of the doctors. He is a short, pudgy guy with caramel skin and bushy hair, who seems smart enough, but when he speaks, his voice is breathy and light, and his sentences remind me of a dog chasing his own tail—a lot of energy spent but only wearing away the same spot in the ground. "The blood results show that your creatinine is decreasing to 2.5," he says, "which is better than what it was, whereas it was 2.8 earlier. So it's good that it's 2.5, but it could be better. But it's definitely better than 2.8, so we'll keep watching it."

After he leaves the room, I always have to ask Charlie to clarify what he said. My father says that part of my confusion is probably because of the fluid I am carrying around. "There is waste in your blood, so it's clouding your brain. You need dialysis to clean up your whole system," he says.

Here we go again, I think. Dialysis is one of the reasons I wanted to get a kidney transplant in the first place. It all comes back now, those mindless hours spent tied to a machine. And that catheter!

Charlie says that I should just do it, that it might help the kidney come back. "And besides," he says, poking at my puffy hips, "it will help you get rid of this weight. I know somewhere in there, my Moonface is still around."

As they wheel me into the procedure room, I tell the anesthesiologist, "Just put me out. I don't want to feel a thing."

I DON'T KNOW WHICH IS MORE LONELY HERE—THE EARLY mornings or the late nights. Nights are maybe easier because, after my parents and Charlie leave, if I'm lucky, I have sleep ahead of me. If I'm lucky, I don't have to be awake for hours. Not until someone wakes me up to draw my blood or take my vitals.

In the morning, I wake up to a gray room and to the sounds of carts, machines, and wheelchairs moving up and down the hall. My father has taped pictures of the Little Bird on the cabinets under the TV to remind me what she looks like, and why I need to get out of here. Mornings are harder maybe because I have to last the whole day long in this place. I've got a whole day of nothing ahead of me.

I am a greedy girl. I should have been thankful enough not just for one transplant but for two. But no, I wanted more. I don't know how I thought I could give birth and get to walk away without a scratch, without putting Birdie, me, or Charlie's kidney in danger. I was living in a fantasyland. It hurts my head to think about that now. The tightness crawls down my neck and over my chest.

"How would you rate your pain?" a nurse, who seems hurried, says late in the morning. I've been up for hours waiting for her. She checks my IV to make sure the anti-rejection medicine is still flowing from the pole.

"Ten," I tell her. "Eleven," I say, just to be sure.

"Let me see what they've ordered for you," she says. She comes back with the syringe and pushes the drug into my IV, and I wait for my shoulders to relax. I let out a groan as the medicine travels through the veins all over my body.

By the time Charlie comes, I am numb to everything—the sounds outside, the smell in the room, the light coming through the blinds. I am so tired that I can barely open my eyes.

"Are you there?" he asks.

"I'm sleepy," I whisper.

"I brought you pho." He holds a clear cylinder steaming with my favorite Vietnamese soup.

"Mmm," I say, slurring, barely moving. "You know it feels good."

"I've brought video of Birdie," Charlie says.

"Mm?" I say before closing my eyes and drifting off, leaving Charlie to spend his entire lunch break with his sleeping wife.

THE TAIL-CHASING DOCTOR COMES IN AND UPDATES ME. I THINK. "Your creatinine has not decreased much from the range it's been holding, and the fevers haven't stopped. We could biopsy you, or give you an ultrasound, or chest x-rays, but a biopsy will tell us what's going on with your kidney. An ultrasound, not so much.

But maybe that would help us determine the origin of the fever. I think a chest x-ray might be good."

"So, is the medicine working or not?" I ask. I just want to understand what the hell he is saying.

"We don't know yet."

"Do you think the kidney is coming back?"

"We'll probably have to do a biopsy eventually to know for sure," he says, though he sounds very unsure.

"So, am I getting a biopsy?"

"Not right now," he says.

"Ultrasound?" I ask. I don't have the energy to fight with him over the tests.

"Yes," he says. "Today."

THE NEXT THING I KNOW, I AM SITTING IN A WHEELCHAIR in nothing but a ghostly hospital gown. They perform ultrasounds in the basement of the hospital, and the waiting room is a weird hallway that seems to exist outside the world, as people, not just patients or hospital staff, cruise past on their way to the cafeteria. Construction crews, bus drivers on breaks, schoolchildren. I watch the waves of people move past me. I wait. And I wait.

The technician who has run tests on me before this recognizes me right away: "I thought you'd be out of here by now."

"Don't get me started," I tell her. She works efficiently, running the same probe over the same area that she did previously. And before too long, I am back in the hall waiting for someone to transport me back to my room.

"Someone will be here to take you up shortly," the receptionist says, pushing my wheelchair closer to the wall.

And now I wait.

A TV in the hall blares a Mexican *telenovela*, which engulfs the voices of some of the other waiting patients. It seems like I've been waiting forever. I clear my throat loudly to get anyone's attention. There are women behind the nurses' station talking about the crab season in Maryland, and I wait, and while I wait, another wave of workers passes me, one of them pushing a tall metal cart of linens with a loose wheel. I think I'm never going to get out of this basement. I think that if I get out of this basement, I could possibly go upstairs, but it doesn't matter because I don't think I will ever get out of this hospital. And that baby, what if that baby never has a mother? What if I died right here in this hospital? I've thought about dying before, of not waking after an operation, of the funeral I might have and who would be there. But this was different. This time, someone—a helpless, lost being—is looking for me, is waiting for me. That is what I am thinking now in this hallway, with the crab discussion happening in the background. I think I could die here, and no one would find me, not my parents, not Birdie, not Charlie. And now I am suddenly aware of my breath, which is sharp, stabbing at my chest, and while I try to slow it down (*deep breath*, I think, *deep breath*), suddenly from my mouth comes the ugliest sound I think I've had ever heard myself make. "*Urgha!*" It wavers in the air like a deflating balloon. And I don't think it was loud enough for anyone but me to hear, but before I know it, it comes out again, louder. Then suddenly, the nurses call out from the desk. "Miss, you all right, miss?"

"When am I getting out of here?"

"Soon, we're just waiting for you to have two more x-rays."

Exactly then, tears stream down my face again, and the crab ladies scramble to find someone to push my chair upstairs.

• • •

WAS THIS A MISTAKE? THAT IS THE QUESTION THAT KEEPS REEMERG-
ing when I sit in the room. When I'm back from the basement and
suddenly back in the bed I've been in for three weeks. I hate myself
for considering this question, for even entertaining the thought.
How can I think that brilliant, shiny little baby could possibly be a
mistake? That she could be anything other than alive, breathing,
and loved in this world? And yet, I think, if I lose this kidney, if I
lose the one thing that Charlie entrusted with me, maybe it was
the wrong decision to get pregnant.

MY FATHER RUSHES INTO THE ROOM. "BABE, YOUR DAUGHTER
is going home!" His eyes are glassy like marbles, and his laugh is
girlish.

"When?" I ask him, trying to smile.

"Today," he says. "Tonight, I should say."

This is good news, I tell myself. She was supposed to stay in the
NICU for three months past her original due date in June. And
now, in the middle of May, she's going out into the world without
me. In a few hours, she'll see our home, the home that Charlie
and I have made for her. The room suddenly gets crowded. Charlie comes in and says, "Did you hear the news?"

"Yes!" I say, feigning excitement.

My mother is on a cell phone with my mother-in-law making
a list of all the things they need to buy before tonight. "Changing
table," she says. "Oh, and diapers, formula . . . Charlie, do you have
any bottles? . . . I will check to see what they use at the NICU."

Charlie and my father make arrangements over keys and
when Charlie will drive her and who will spend the night helping
him. A nurse comes in to check on my IV fluids. I watch them all
from my bed, and I want it all to stop. I don't want Birdie to go

home without me. I want to be there. I want the world to stop until I get out of here. If I get out of here.

THEY LEAVE IN A HURRY, KISSING ME ON THE FOREHEAD ON THEIR way out. "I'll be right back," Charlie says. "I'm just going to install the car seat. But I'll be back before I pick her up."

As soon as he leaves, I press the call button and tell the nurse on duty that I am in pain. I just want that feeling in my shoulders again.

When Charlie comes back, I'm out of it again.

"Did you take another one of those pain meds?" he asks.

I nod.

"Hello? Can you even speak?" he says, his jaw tensing up. "Enough of this. No more."

He presses the call button and asks to see my nurse. I hear him tell her that I can't have any more of this medicine. He won't allow it.

"It's written in the doctor's orders," the nurse says.

"I'm her husband, and I'm telling you it's making her crazy," he says.

BIRDIE HAS BEEN HOME FOR FOUR DAYS. SHE HAS HAD A PARADE of visitors, and my parents tell me that my niece Genevieve has tied pink balloons all along our brick porch to celebrate her arrival.

Charlie reports back from the first ride home from the hospital with his baby girl in the backseat. He says he is convinced that 65 percent of the drivers on the road are completely drunk and trying to kill him and his daughter. A guy nearly sideswiped her side of the car on Roland Avenue, he says, and I imagine Charlie taking big, exaggerated turns so the car doesn't come near the curb, and I picture him driving cautiously slow, like an old man, down a busy street with the cars honking at him, unmoved by other drivers' curses and gestures. He says he got her home safely, and with his mother's help, learned how to spend the night giving the Little Bird tiny bottle feedings every few hours.

I am happy that he is learning the ropes, but I am so jealous. Even though I know I am alive, I feel like I am dead. I feel like I died in childbirth, and Birdie will grow up to be one of those motherless children who has to be raised by someone other than the woman who gave birth to her. What good is a mother if she is not there, if she misses those vital first days? Birdie needs to come home, but I do not want her there without me.

This illness is making me selfish. Shouldn't a mother be selfless? Shouldn't a mother want what is best for her child? This illness is making me cruel. Is this the person I have become?

THE DOCTOR WHO SPEAKS IN WHISPERS AND CIRCLES HAS STOPPED coming around, and another doctor—a young, good-looking Chinese man—enters the picture. Before he speaks, he walks into my room in his lab coat one night and paces back and forth by the foot of my bed. He rattles the change in his pockets. Behind him, a fluorescent light is shining on Birdie's picture, her little face.

"I'm feeling a little pessimistic about this kidney coming back," he says. He stops his pacing and looks at me squarely across the bed. "I think we've tried everything we can."

At first, when I hear his words, I only feel relief. I am losing Charlie's kidney and the first thing I think is: *Let it go.* I can feel my shoulders fall.

"You're young, you're a new mom. You're the perfect candidate for another transplant, so I'm confident you'll get one."

"I don't even want to think about a transplant right now," I tell him. "I just want to get home to my baby."

"Understandable. But, really, you should. You're not going to want to be a mother and have to go on dialysis. I'm going to recommend you to the transplant coordinator."

Transplant, coordinator, list, whatever. I can't conceive of a transplant right now. I can't quite yet conceive the idea of someone replacing Charlie's kidney.

I TELL CHARLIE THE NEWS WHEN HE COMES IN THAT EVENING.

"About time," he says. Then he stands up and lifts the bedding off my legs. "Let's go!"

"Wait, they're getting my paperwork. They're trying to find a dialysis center for me to go to." I'm excited to go home, but when I say this, it hits me what else I'm going home to. "Dialysis again, Charlie."

"It might be temporary. Maybe the kidney will kick back. And if not, remember, you've got a baby girl waiting for you. She needs you right now. And dialysis—we'll get through it." He stands there already looking exhausted, yet undaunted by what's ahead.

"Who's going to take care of her while I'm at my treatments? How am I going to get to dialysis? We'll need lots of help. I'll need help just holding her."

"I don't care what it takes," Charlie says. "I just want my Moonface back."

Chapter Seventeen

The ORNITHOLOGICAL WONDER in the SPHERE of POSSIBILITY

• • •

I AM ALMOST SCARED OF HER. MY PARENTS DRIVE ME HOME FROM the hospital, and I walk into the house that night with all my clothes in a plastic bag. The balloons Genevieve had strung along our porch for Birdie's homecoming are now deflated and barely hanging above the ground. There are packages addressed to "Nico Carmen O'Doyle" on the porch. This person gets mail. She owns things. She probably has a checkbook.

Inside, I feel like I have just missed the party, that the main attraction has come and gone. There are more boxes on the living room floor filled with tiny outfits with the tags still attached. The dog is asleep on gift-wrapping paper.

Still overweight with fluid, I cannot yet carry my weight gracefully. But I make my way upstairs, with my father's help.

"One step," he says, one of his hands holding mine and the other one under my elbow. "Another step. Slow, babe, one step at a time."

When I get to the top of the stairs, I see her nursery that we had painted bright orange and the crib that I had begged Charlie to assemble for months. He finally put it together one Sunday, and three days later, Birdie was born. Once, in the hospital, he said, "See, I should have waited ten more weeks."

Her room is filled with our moving boxes that have never been unpacked, a desk, a file cabinet. Her room is not yet hers.

OUR BEDROOM IS BLUE, AND IT GLOWS WITH A SOFT READING light in the corner. Next to the bed is the small bassinet in which someone has laid out a soft pink flannel blanket. And on the bed, Charlie lies down on his side and curls up next to Birdie's small mound. She sleeps with her nose pressed to his arm.

"Here she is! There is Mommy!" he whispers. I am scared I will make her cry, or that she will not remember me, or that maybe I am someone different now than on the day she was born. Maybe twenty-six days apart has made us strangers. But when I slide in next to her, there it is: that face! Her eyes are tiny bulges still, bubbles on her skin. Her lips are thin folds, moist with milk. Her nose is enormous compared with the rest of her features. She breathes so quietly. I hold her under her neck and under her diaper, and set her head against my chest. She rolls her face back and forth into my skin, but she does not cry.

My parents' feet are creaking on the floorboards downstairs as they escape and let us be alone together. I hold her for as long as I can before she gets hungry, and then Charlie and I spend the rest of the night hunched over her bassinet like two kids looking into a box of baby chicks.

• • •

CHARLIE HAS TO GO TO WORK THE NEXT MORNING, AND HE TELLS me that someone will be here to help me with the baby, but they won't arrive until ten or so.

"Who will it be?" I ask him.

"I don't know. The grandmothers have it worked out."

He is supposed to leave at eight, so I have two hours of being a mother on my own, though I don't know where to begin. Charlie teaches me her morning routine. He teaches me how to be a mother. He gave her the three and six o'clock feedings the night before, and I watched him, now an adept father, hold her head in the crook of his arm and put the tiny bottle gingerly to her lips.

"Bottles first," he says, taking little prepackaged bottles from a shopping bag and placing them on the nightstand. "She's up to ten CCs of formula. Isn't that great?"

"Yes!" I say, trying to remember how many CCs she drank in the hospital. The truth is that I don't know how much better ten CCs of formula is than what she had at the hospital. When I left her, she wasn't yet drinking from a bottle.

"Just make sure she finishes the whole amount. She's almost five pounds, Moonface. She's getting up there. I've been telling her she's got to drink more. I say to her, 'What if you grow up and you want to be a lawyer? What are you going to do? Be a five-pound lawyer all your life? Who's going to hire a five-pound lawyer?'"

I picture our Little Bird in a tiny business suit, toddling around on skinny legs, and holding the smallest attaché imaginable. Just then, she farts loudly into my hand.

"Oh, and she farts a lot," Charlie chuckles. "A chip off the old stinky block. Now here's how you swaddle her," Charlie says. "We've got all these blankets that the NICU sent us home with. The nurses said that Birdie feels better when she's swaddled because it simulates the womb."

"I hope it's a more welcoming womb than mine," I say under my breath.

"I don't think it was your womb that was the problem, Debbie Downer. Now watch. You go like this." He lays out a blanket in a folded triangle. "Here," he says, reaching for our baby. I pass her to him, and the hand-off is awkward. "You put her in here." He gently places her in the middle of the upside-down triangle, and then folds one end over the other.

"That's too tight," I say.

"No, she likes it." Then he hands her back to me. Her lips begin to suckle, then relax. She is still asleep and having tiny baby dreams.

"Onward! Diapers! Our moms bought a changing table. It's ugly, but we can buy another one later. Come in here."

He walks toward her room, and Birdie and I follow. She is lying across my arms, her neck on the inside of my elbow. I trail behind Charlie, and I forget that the doorway that leads to her room is narrow. As we pass through, her head knocks against the wooden doorframe and she lets out the cry of a squeaky toy being stepped on. I don't want Charlie to hear what I've done so I cough and clear my throat until she stops.

"You okay?" he says.

"Yup," I say, holding her head to ease her pain.

The table is ugly and not what I have dreamed for her nursery, but on it, Charlie shows me how to put the diapers on her and how to sponge bathe her. As he gives me instructions on how he prefers to do things, I think I could be the babysitter right now, the one getting the run-through of what to do while the parents are gone.

I am scared when he leaves.

"You'll be fine," Charlie says.

I nod.

"It's easy. Just be with her. That's all you have to do. One of our mothers will be here by ten, so you'll have help. They'll know what to do."

After he leaves, I lay her down on our bed and we sleep until help arrives.

IT'S A FRIDAY, SO I HAVE THE WEEKEND TO REST AND BE WITH her until my dialysis treatments start on Monday. I lie down in the bed beside her, but my mind doesn't rest trying to put the pieces of this bleak picture together. My parents have practically moved into the hotel down the street, but soon they'll have to get back home to Pennsylvania. They will have to get back to their own lives. My mother-in-law lives an hour away, but she has not yet retired from her job. Charlie has taken so many days off over the past weeks. I still can't drive because of my wound and the cumbersome fluid under my skin. I can't bring Birdie to my treatments with me. Right now, we are two needy babies; neither of us can fend for herself.

She is five pounds, but I still lift her with some effort. A lump in my arms. Because my trunk and my legs are still so watered down, I can't navigate my body like I used to before I was pregnant. In the mornings, when it's time to make a bottle for her, I hold her and we practically slide down the stairs together, my back pressed against the wall for support. Slowly we go, sidestepping the whole staircase. Our nights are broken up into three-hour intervals, and for every feeding I try to lift her out of the bassinet, almost pulling her body across the soft edge and onto our bed.

I have a dream one night. I dream that I am wading in water. It must be an ocean, but the water seems more brown than blue.

There is a pier extending from the beach. I can't see Charlie or Birdie, just some men on the shore. One man has long hair and a beard. A wave rises and falls. But then another wave comes and it does not stop. I try to hold my ground, but it just keeps coming, and it seems like the rush of water is never going to end. *When will this wave break?* I think to myself, as I push against the water with my arms so my head doesn't go under. The man with the beard calls out, "Duck out, everyone!" I know at that moment that this is a tsunami and that this wave will probably not break anytime soon. My eyes must be filled with panic because the man with the beard reaches over to me, grabs my hand, and says, "This way!" We swim underneath the pier in search of an air pocket or somewhere to breathe. Soon we are underwater, and I am holding my breath. All I can see is the brown water and sand particles floating past. I am waiting for us to come up for air. Waiting, waiting, being guided by this man's hand the whole time. I'm not sure if we never come up for air or if I wake up before we have a chance to.

IN THE MORNING, I SIT UP AGAINST THE HEADBOARD BEFORE Charlie wakes.

"You okay?" he says as he stretches and yawns. "Is it nine o'clock already?" He looks over me and into Birdie's bassinet. "Is she breathing?"

I shake my head, but not at his question. "I just can't believe it. I can't believe I'm on dialysis again. I can't believe the kidney failed. How did this happen?" I say.

"Well," Charlie says, pulling himself upright, "you'd better believe it. You're on dialysis for now. You've got to accept it, Moony. I feel bad about it. I'm so sorry."

"Why are you sorry?" I say. "*I'm* sorry."

"Because my kidney didn't make it. The little German didn't pull through. It's a shame."

"But that's not your fault," I tell him.

"Yeah, well, it's not your fault either. It just happened. Things have to happen to make room for other things." He stretches and yawns again, still trying to wake up.

I am not consoled. Why can't things just happen and everything be healthy and well for once? I want to say this out loud, but I know that he doesn't want to hear it.

"Think about it this way," he says. "What is the best thing that ever happened to us?"

"Birdie." I say it quickly. Then I think back on every little thing that has happened to us. Every trip, every dance, every kiss. The answer is the same. "Birdie."

"I'd say the same thing: Birdie," he agrees, looking into her bassinet just in case she hears us talking about her. "And if it weren't for my kidney in your body, then she wouldn't be here. If you didn't have that kidney from the moment she was conceived to the moment she was born, there would be no Birdie. The little German did exactly what he needed to do. Unfortunately, he wasn't interested in overtime."

"I guess, Charlie. And she's brilliant and perfect. Even growing in my weird-ass, messed-up body. But with the dialysis and all, I guess I'm just surprised about how it all turned out."

"Surprised? Really, Moonface?" he says, seeming surprised himself by my answer. "Our life has been nothing but an endless stream of things going differently than we imagined. Don't you think?" he says.

"For real," I say.

"You know what it's like?" he says. He gets up on his knees in the bed. "It's like a circus that goes horribly wrong. Or a variety show full of bombs. It's one spectacle after another. Thank god you're always here so I can follow your cues."

"My cues?" I say, a little confused. "I thought I was the straight man."

"What?" he says, looking confused. "I thought I was the straight man." He points at his chest.

"No, I am."

"No, me," he says, digging his nose into my neck.

I pull his body closer. "I'll give you a cue to follow," I say, grabbing his face and kissing his lips. I scream when he tries to bite my face and we almost wake the baby.

THE ENTIRE FAMILY IS HELPING US. MY MOTHER-IN-LAW COMES and stays with Birdie every other afternoon while I'm at my treatments. Sometimes, my parents drive four hours to be with her. And Charlie sometimes leaves his job early, and his bosses understand.

It's a complicated and taxing situation. But maybe my dialysis schedule will become more convenient. Maybe the little German will eventually pull through. There are reasons to think it might. A nurse at the dialysis center tells me to hold on—she's seen one guy's kidney bounce back after six months on dialysis. "He was there one day, and then we never saw him again," she tells me.

Most days after the treatments, I'm tired and I just want to come home and sleep beside Birdie. Thankfully, she sleeps as much as I do in a day. On the days I have off, though, I have more energy and a clearer mind. I stare at her all day, feed her bottles, change her diapers, sing her songs. I do the things that a mother should do. I like to take off her Onesie sometimes and just look at her bare body. I hold my hand against her chest and feel her heart beating, her chest rising and falling, her fingers wrapping around my thumb, and all her parts moving and working. I like to think that maybe I am sick so she doesn't have to be, that maybe somewhere in the pregnancy, I took it all for her. That something magical transcended the umbilical cord, the uterus, all of it. And for that reason, I would do it over and over and over again for her. I hold my breath so she can breathe.

ONE DAY, I COME HOME FROM DIALYSIS AND CHARLIE IS ON THE couch with her. Birdie is dressed in an outfit that Charlie has picked out, and I take one look at it and know that I have to change her immediately, because no baby of mine will be seen in a bright orange Onesie and purple pants.

"She's a trendsetter," Charlie protests.

Her delicate bones resist ever so slightly when I slide them into sleeves and through leg holes of tiny pants. She pushes my hand away when I try to fasten a snap on her Onesie. These days, Charlie and I wait for her to open her eyes because she keeps them open only for short periods of time. The minute she looks up at us, we call out, "Open!"

I tell Charlie she looks like me: "Everyone is saying so. Same hair, same eyes, same nose." Birdie lies between us on the bed. She is sleeping with her tiny hand against her cheek.

"Ah, but those eyebrows," Charlie says. "They are all me."

She opens her mouth a sliver and lets out a squeak.

"Oh, here's our five-pound lawyer now," Charlie says. As she cries, he says, "You know what she's saying?"

"What?"

"She's saying, 'Your Honor, I object! . . . Strenuously!'" He uses a child's pouty voice. He pulls her near by her tiny torso, and she squirms into his chest.

"You should set your goals higher for her," I tell him. "Maybe she'll be a judge."

"A sixteen-inch judge . . . I like it."

"Yeah, or the world's smallest acrobat."

"Or the pint-sized math prodigy."

"Or the knee-high ninja."

She continues to squirm, so I take her from Charlie and hold her in my arms. Her eyes open now. "Open!" we say. We show her who her mama is and who her dada is. We point to the dog, and the lamp, and the pictures of her on the nightstand, and the pillows, and the bassinet. Her eyes do not seem frightened or worried. They are wide and bright, and they are filled with the wonder of it all.

EPILOGUE

· · ·

I N THE BEDROOM OF OUR SECOND-STORY HOME, CHARLIE AND I lie in bed and watch old black-and-white footage of vaudeville shows from the early 1900s. It's an extensive variety of the strangest performances. A giant and a dwarf do a synchronized tap dance with rifles before the dwarf clocks the giant in the knee. An Asian elephant jumps rope with a Border collie. A man and woman play dueling ukuleles and then kiss. We don't watch old vaudeville footage often, but when we do, I don't know whether they are funny or sad, whether I'm supposed to be amused by these performances or shocked by them. One thing's for certain: I can't look away.

"You don't *want* to look away," Charlie says. "You might miss the punch line."

"And it just doesn't stop," I tell him. "One after the other. The acts just keep coming to the stage, one more obscure than the one before."

"This one." Charlie points to the screen. A dog is setting a table for dinner. Charlie starts to cackle, pumping his arms up and down as he breathes.

"Shh!" I say. "You'll wake the bird." Birdie lies between us in bed, her face mashed into the sheets. She is almost two now, her body still thin and resembling an older version of that two-pound baby in the NICU. But now, her face has filled out, and there are bulges on her cheeks on which one can squeeze her. I am one of those bad mothers who still co-sleeps, putting my nose against her face on the mattress as we drift to sleep. I just can't bear to have her far from me.

The only other time after her birth that we were separated was almost a year ago. And I didn't mind leaving her in the capable arms of her father; I was busy getting healthy.

Maggie, my friend from grad school who was willing to give her kidney to a stranger, called me three months after Birdie was born. She had ignored all advice about donating before getting inseminated, and started the donation process in Iowa. Thank god for her stubbornness because the hospital in Iowa did not yet know what to do with altruistic donations, and they did not know what to do with her information. They ran the tests and held her records. Meanwhile, she heard that I was having a hard time on dialysis and getting back in shape.

She called and said, "If I'm going to give up my kidney, I'm not going to give it to a stranger when I can give it to you."

So, a little under a year to the day that Birdie was born, Maggie flew from Iowa to Baltimore, and we checked ourselves into the university hospital. We were a sight, in our O.R. caps, our paper gowns, our hospital footsies, and our loud support team surrounding us in the surgical prep area: Charlie, my parents, Beth, Maggie's wife, her mom. Maggie's mom held her hand and mine in a particularly touching but silent moment. My dad tried to take a picture, standing way back in the corner of the room, and shouted, "I can't make us all fit!" We laughed, hurdling over each other, over my gurney and Maggie's, trying to fit in the frame. It was so loud and silly and we were all laughing so hard, we almost cried.

Maggie and I checked in on a Tuesday, and by Monday, she and her wife were back on a plane to Iowa. My kidney function was perfect by the time she left, but because of another pesky fever and discomfort around the wound site, I almost didn't make it home in time for Birdie's first birthday.

"She won't even notice," Charlie assured me. "She kind of goes by her own schedule anyhow. I'll tell her you're just waiting for your guts to move my kidney out of the way to make room for Maggie's."

Still, I begged the surgeons to send me home, crying into my hands unapologetically. Charlie got me home at 3:30 p.m. on the first anniversary of her birth, and together, we helped our baby blow out her first birthday candle.

Charlie keeps saying that measurements don't really count anymore, but to me they still do. I wanted to be there for her first birthday, I count the pounds she gains between office visits, and I write down how many minutes her naps last. Sometimes I calculate how long this new kidney might last. Maggie and I keep hoping that this one will last forever. Maggie is not a blood relative, and we are not each other's one true love. But, unlike my other donors, she is a girl this time, and maybe that will be the magical element between us. I make up these possibilities despite knowing that this little kidney has as much chance as the others did, that we can expect it to hold out for ten or so years, provided no problems get in the way. I calculate what Birdie will be doing in ten years, and I wonder if she'll be taking care of me or if I'll still be able to take care of her.

"What difference does it make in ten years?" Charlie always says when my mind wanders. "She needs you *now*."

Back in bed, Birdie stirs in her sleep.

"You're too loud," I tell Charlie. He clicks off the TV right when an attractive woman starts to undress. "Oh, too bad," I say, laughing at his unfortunate timing.

"I don't need no stinkin' TV to see burlesque," he says. He grabs at my shirt, and I squeal as I try to push him away. The dog hears the commotion and jumps on the bed with a yelp, waking the sleeping baby, who now opens the deep dark cavern of her mouth widely and lets out a bloodcurdling yell.

"No stinkin' TV," I yell to Charlie. "All the entertainment you need is right here."

ACKNOWLEDGMENTS

. . .

Thanks to Rakesh Satyal for your unending patience and your faith in this book. Thanks to my agent, Dan Lazar, for fighting for me, especially when I was too sick to do so myself. I realize it is difficult to be astute businessmen while still having warm, generous hearts, and yet both of you seem to do this without compromise.

Thanks to my parents, Angel B. Balcita Jr. and Dolores P. Balcita, for innumerable sacrifices. Thank you for your big, enormous, and smothering love. I can't imagine the person I would be without it.

Thanks to Joel and Karla Balcita, for always being there ready to help. You made many days so much easier.

Thanks to Kim, Jean, Wes, Claire, Genevieve, and Alexandra and the rest of the Doyle family, for your support and enthusiastic encouragement.

Thanks to the good people at the 25th Street DaVita Dialysis

Center in Baltimore, the Johns Hopkins Hospital, and the University of Iowa Hospitals and Clinics.

My deepest gratitude to the readers and advisors who read drafts, offered direction, and cheered me on during the writing process: Suzanne Guillette, Heal McKnight, Maggie McKnight, Lynne Nugent, Amber Withycombe, Kembrew McLeod, Megan Knight, Kerry Reilly, Sarah Courteau, Bonnie J. Rough, Jynelle Gracia, Danielle O'Hare, Melissa Hartman, Karen Henoch-Ryugo, Michelle Muratori, Kristi Birch, Iryna Pustovoyt, and Amy Thompson.

Thanks to the Haven Foundation, PEN American Center, the American Society of Journalists and Authors Charitable Trust, the Kimmel Harding Nelson Center for the Arts, Fine Arts Work Center in Provincetown, and the University of Iowa for your invaluable and generous support.

Thanks to the *New York Times* and the *Iowa Review*.

Thanks to everyone at HarperCollins for the care you took with this book.

Thanks to my incredible teachers: David Hamilton, Robin Hemley, Susan Lohafer, Patricia Foster, Gerry Albarelli, and Ron Tanner.

Thank you, Nico Carmen Birdie Cutie-Pie Baby-Baby Boochie Doyle, for being more than we could have ever imagined. When I look at you, I see only the many reasons there are to create and to dream.

And lastly, thank you, Christopher K. Doyle, for making the otherwise tragic seem magnificent and extraordinary. Down into the easy chair we go . . .